CHANGING BRITAIN

ON THE BREADLINE

ALAN EVANS

B.T. Batsford Ltd · London

First published 1994

Typeset by Goodfellow & Egan
Phototypesetting Ltd, Cambridge

and printed in Singapore

Published by
B.T. Batsford Ltd
4 Fitzhardinge Street
London W1H 0AH

A catalogue record for this book is
available from the British Library

ISBN 0 7134 6715 0

British Coinage before Decimalization

Until 1970, when decimal currency was adopted, the pound
was divided into shillings. There were twenty shillings to the
pound and twelve pence to the shilling.

old money	abbreviation	value in new pence*
one penny	1d	less than ½p
sixpence	6d	2½p
half a crown	2s 6d or 2/6d	12½p
ten shillings	10s or 10/-	50p

* Remember that prices are now higher than in the past
because of inflation.

This book examines the problem of poverty in Britain over the last century. But what does the word 'poverty' mean? The dictionary defines it as 'being poor, suffering a great lack of money and resources' and the playwright George Bernard Shaw was no doubt correct when he wrote that 'The greatest of evils and the worst of crimes is poverty.'

However, a sense of outrage at the existence of poverty in Britain is something quite recent. For most people in this country until the twentieth century, poverty was the normal condition of life and was not a 'problem' at all. In the Bible, St John writes: 'The poor always ye have with you.' Nearly two thousand years later, in the mid-nineteenth century, the hymn writer Mrs C. Alexander composed these famous words:

> The rich man at his castle,
> The poor man at his gate,
> God made them, high or lowly,
> And order'd their estate.

For hundreds of years it was widely believed that, for many people, poverty was not only inevitable but was part of God's plan for mankind. Jesus particularly loved the poor, saying 'It is easier for a camel to go through the eye of a needle, than for a rich man to enter into the Kingdom of God.' Of course, to derive comfort from this teaching, one must believe that life on earth is just a prelude to the afterlife, and even devout Christians might feel today that this alone offers cold comfort to the poor. However, in the nineteenth century and before, the well-to-do believed that poverty was something brought about simply by the personal failings of the poor. Because they were idle or drunken or spendthrifts they brought their poverty upon themselves.

For the historian there are many difficulties in studying poverty. It is easy to condemn harsh attitudes of the past, but we also have to try to understand why people held these views. Then there is the difficulty of comparing poverty across centuries – can we compare the lot of the poor man in 1890 with that of a poor man in 1990? Is there, in other words, an absolute standard of poverty and if there is, what is it? Or is all poverty relative, since the poor man only feels deprived when at the castle gate of the rich man?

For those faced with the task of dealing with the poor, in our time and in the past, there is the difficulty of distinguishing between the 'deserving' poor (those who want to work and support themselves but are unable to, including such groups as the sick, the elderly, orphans and widows) and the 'undeserving' poor (those who will not work or have made themselves poor because of their foolish habits). And how is poverty to be treated: by providing for the basic needs of the poor or by removing its causes? This in turn begs other questions: what are the basic needs of the poor at any time? What are the causes of poverty?

The questions increase, the answers become more difficult, just as the task of eradicating poverty in Britain has so far proved impossible.

Yet over the last century in Britain (and in the western world generally) poverty has come to be seen as a soluble problem, not part of the natural condition of mankind. The Industrial Revolution from the late eighteenth century on has held out the prospect of plenty, not just for the powerful but for all. It is this increasing material wealth which has made solving the problem of poverty possible, whilst at the same time making it increasingly hard to define it and to destroy it for good. Thus we continually see newspaper headlines and stories telling us about 'the poverty trap', 'the North–South divide', the growth of an 'underclass' of alienated, poor young people begging in the streets of London and so on. Yet it could be argued that no one in late twentieth-century Britain is really poor, not by the standards of a hundred years ago, and that increasing wealth has led to increasingly generous state handouts, which in turn lead to people 'opting-out' of society, believing that they have a right to be cared for by the state 'from cradle to grave' without any corresponding duties on their part.

By the time you have read this book you should be in a position to start working out your attitudes to the problems that lie behind the words 'the problem of poverty'.

The year 1834 was a turning-point in the social history of England. The Poor Law Amendment Act of that year overturned the existing poor-relief system (what historians call the 'Old Poor Law') and introduced the 'New Poor Law' that was to last for over a century. Before 1834 the way the poor were dealt with was laid down by two Acts of Parliament dating from the late sixteenth century. These Acts created a poor-relief system based on the 15,000 parishes of England and Wales. Well-to-do people in each parish had to pay a poor rate each year, which provided help for the 'deserving poor' (i.e. widows, orphans, the sick and elderly), usually while they continued to live in their own homes. The able-bodied were given financial help or food and clothing only after they had helped repair the local roads or had done some work (like weaving cloth) in the local House of Correction. Under an important act of 1662 paupers could only be helped in the parish they were born in. Behind this system of poor relief were three principles. First, if the poor were not helped there might be riots and even perhaps revolution. Second, the able-bodied poor would benefit themselves (and others) if they were made to work. Third was the widely held belief that the fortunate should help the less fortunate.

It was this method for dealing with the poor, modified by the 1795 allowance (or Speenhamland) system, subsidizing the wages of farm workers from the poor rates, that was abolished in 1834. Rate-payers had been complaining for some years of the growing expense of helping the poor (£2 million in 1785, £8½ million in 1821) and riots by agricultural labourers in southern England in 1830 led many to believe that the poor were neither grateful for, nor

being improved by, the aid they were receiving. The government set up a Royal Commission in 1832 to examine the way the poor-relief system worked, and the recommendations it put forward in 1834, which were mainly the ideas of Edwin Chadwick, were the basis of the 1834 Poor Law Amendment Act.

Under the Act local Boards of Guardians, elected by the rate-payers, were to run the New Poor Law. Parishes were grouped into about 700 Poor Law unions and each union was to have a workhouse. Super-vising the whole system from London were three Poor Law Commissioners. The workhouse was central to the new system and between 1834 and 1883 a massive investment of around £13 million went into building these institutions, which it was intended should have a forbidding reputation. All those who claimed poor relief were to be sent to their union workhouse. The guiding principle behind the running of the workhouses was that of 'less eligibility', i.e. conditions there were deliberately to be made worse than in the outside world so as to discourage all but the desperate from entering them. This 'workhouse test' would thus reduce the cost of the Poor Law system. The workhouses were built to look like prisons and, inside, the sexes, including husbands and wives, were separated. Different age groups were kept apart and children were taken from their mothers as soon as they could walk. To make matters worse, the routine of the workhouse was one of paralysing boredom. The diet was such that the inmates knew with dreary certainty what they would eat for the rest of their stay, which for the

elderly could mean the rest of their lives. The paupers were dressed in prison-like uniforms; some unions put their unmarried mothers into a bright-yellow dress, yellow being the colour of the quarantine flag flown by ships infested with the plague. Children had their hair cut close to the scalp and were allowed no toys. Able-bodied men had to carry out jobs like bone-crushing, grinding glass or breaking stones. Able-bodied women cleaned the workhouse, washed the clothes of the inmates and acted as nurses. Edwin Chadwick wrote much of the 1834 report and played a large part in running the new system in the mid-1830s. He justified this regime in the following way: 'It [the work-house] is like a cold bath; unpleasant in contemplation but invigorating in its effects.'

In practice, however, the Poor Law Commission was never able to run a system in which all paupers were kept in workhouses. It has been estimated that only about 10–20% of paupers ever saw the inside of a workhouse in the mid-nineteenth century. This was partly because of the kindliness of local Boards of Guardians and partly because it was cheaper to provide help for a poor family outside the workhouse than inside it. A second problem was that early Victorian Britain was in many ways a brutal society. Sports like bull-baiting and dog-fighting were popular, murderers were hung in public, and soldiers and sailors flogged for disciplinary offences. The inmates of the workhouses were in fact often enjoying a better standard of living, 'less eligibility' not withstanding, than many on the

The workhouses were built to look like prisons

even-bleaker outside.

However, working people, who often spent part or all of their lives in poverty or in danger of falling into poverty, hated the New Poor Law, even though its cruelty was psychological rather than physical. Many would not even use the word 'workhouse' and instead spoke of 'the union' or 'the Bastille' or ironically of 'the pauper palace'. As the poet George Crabbe wrote early in the nineteenth century:

> It is a prison, with a milder name, which few inhabit without dread or shame.

This dread lasted until recent years. One historian, writing of her childhood in the 1950s in London's Notting Hill, tells of how people still thought of the local hospital (which had originally been a workhouse infirmary) as a place of 'hopelessness, coercion, death . . .'

Yet from the point of view of Parliament, government and rate-payers the New Poor Law was a success. In the three decades after 1834, and despite a rapidly growing population, the cost of poor relief was kept down. Expenditure did increase in the 1860s, but then the principles of 1834 were strongly reasserted and costs were again kept strictly under control for most of the rest of the century.

Women working inside a workhouse in the early nineteenth century. How is the principle of less eligibility being put into operation?

The Principle of Deterrence

I wish to see the poor house looked to with dread by our labouring classes and the reproach for being an inmate of it extend downwards from father to son. Let the poor see and feel that their parish, although it will not allow them to perish through absolute want, is yet the hardest taskmaster, the closest paymaster and the most harsh and unkind friend they can apply to.

Captain George Nicholls writing about the experimental workhouse he set up in the 1820s in Southwell, Nottinghamshire. Nicholls became one of the first three Poor Law Commissioners.

Nicholls was an ex-sea captain and a self-made man. Can you explain why this might have made him unsympathetic to the poor? How did Nicholls see his workhouse deterring the poor from claiming help from the parish?

The Daily Routine in the Workhouse

From 25 March to 29 September the paupers are to rise at 5 a.m.

6 a.m.	morning prayers and breakfast
7 a.m. to 12 noon	work in the labour yard
12 noon to 1 p.m.	dinner
1 p.m. to 7 p.m.	labour yard
7 p.m.	supper followed by evening prayers
8 p.m.	the paupers are to retire to bed and all candles are to be extinguished

From 30 September to 24 March the paupers are to rise at 7 a.m.

An extract from an order issued by the Poor Law Commission in the late 1830s.

How would this daily routine have deterred those considering claiming poor relief? Note that on Sundays there was no work but compulsory chapel attendance.

Workhouse Diets

Breakfasts – 7 oz. bread, 1½ pints gruel or porridge. Dinners – Sundays, 5 oz. meat and ¾ lb. vegetables; Thursdays, ditto; Mondays, 1½ pints soup and 7 oz. vegetables; Fridays, ditto; Tuesdays, 14 oz. rice or suet pudding; Wednesdays, 7 oz. bread and 2 oz. cheese. Suppers – Sundays, Tuesdays and Thursdays, 7 oz. bread and 2 oz. cheese. Other nights, ¾ lb. potatoes.

Breakfasts – 6 oz. bread, 1 oz. cheese. Dinners – Sundays, 16 oz. suet pudding; Mondays, 6 oz. bread, 1 oz cheese; Tuesdays and Thursdays, 4 oz. meat, ¾ lb. potatoes, yeast dumpling; Wednesdays and Saturdays, bread and cheese, as Mondays; Fridays, 11 oz. meat dumpling. Supper, 6 oz. bread, 1 oz. cheese, 1 pint broth.

Two sample menus provided by the Poor Law Commission in 1836. Unions could choose which to follow.

Examine the diets carefully. Is one more generous than the other? How do they compare in quantity and variety of food with what you eat in a week?

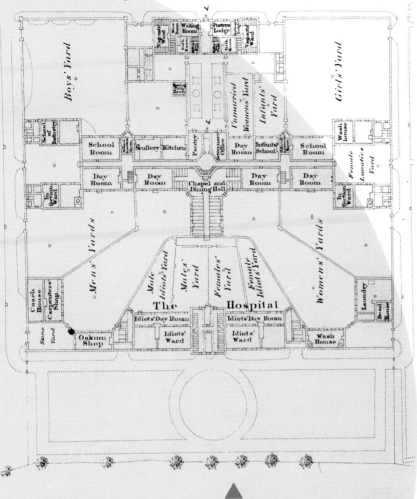

A typical workhouse of the nineteenth century. How does the plan put into effect the principles of deterrence and 'less eligibility'?

What do you think these men are doing?

1 Using this book and any other information you may have, write an account of a day in the workhouse. You could imagine that you are a workhouse child or an able-bodied pauper.

2 Try to find a copy in your school or local public library of Charles Dickens's famous novel *Oliver Twist*. Chapter 2 contains a description of a workhouse child asking for more food. Do you think this is a fair comment on the post-1834 Poor Law system? What are the benefits and pit-falls of using novels as historical evidence? Other books by Dickens that shed light on the workhouses of the time are *Little Dorrit* (chapter 31), *Our Mutual Friend* (book I, chapter 16 and book II, chapter 8) and *The Uncommercial Traveller* (a collection of his writings, see chapter 3).

3 The men who framed the New Poor Law's provisions were not wicked or cruel. Can you explain in your own words what they were trying to achieve?

The workhouses, renamed 'Poor Law Institutions' in 1913, dominated the landscape of Victorian England. Today the workhouse is seen as a symbol of the heartlessness of Victorian attitudes to poverty, yet despite the fact that the 1834 Act was a response by Parliament to the demands of public opinion, or at least rate-payer opinion, many nineteenth-century men and women attacked the workhouse and all it stood for. Agricultural labourers in southern England in the mid-1830s rioted against the new system of poor relief, and the more organized anti-Poor-Law movement in the manufacturing districts of the North developed into Chartism at the end of the 1830s. At the same time in Parliament, some MPs, including the young Benjamin Disraeli, who was later to be a Conservative prime minister, spoke out against the cruelty of the workhouse system and its interference in local affairs. Middle-class newspapers and magazines like *The Times* and *Punch* also attacked the workhouses, as did writers such as Dickens and, later, Thomas Hardy. In the face of such protests, and of revelations of cruelty in some workhouses, for example in Andover in Hampshire in the 1840s, the system was modified. Thus in 1844 it was agreed that outdoor relief could be given at times of sudden trade slumps in industrial areas, and in 1847 married couples over the age of sixty were allowed to share a room. Local Boards of Guardians proved so willing to give poor relief without forcing paupers into the workhouse that only a small proportion of those claiming relief even entered a 'Bastille'. Yet although the middle-class opponents of the workhouse were loud in their complaints, they had no real alternative to offer, especially as far as the able-bodied poor were concerned.

Moreover, the workhouse system operated uneasily alongside another Victorian value: belief in private charity. The harshness of the Poor Law almost certainly encouraged charitable giving, which in any case was an obligation laid on the well-to-do by custom and by religious duty. Thus William Gladstone, the Liberal Prime Minister, devoted a large part of his wealth to charity, giving one-eleventh of his income while an undergraduate at Oxford, and an average of one-eighth for the years 1831–40. In 1885 he calculated that, since 1831, he had given £52,113 to 'Charity and Religion'. As a deeply religious man, Gladstone believed that ultimately he would be answerable to God for the use he had made during his lifetime of his wealth. Although Gladstone did not advertise his charitable giving, other wealthy Victorians did, and their names were emblazoned on buildings, statues and in the press. To be known as a philanthropist was to gain public respect. A survey of 446 wills has shown that £20 million was given to charity in the 1890s by wealthy individuals. At the other end of the scale there were countless donations by individuals to such things as the 'poor box' at Marylebone Police Court in London, which provided 2,000 people each year with soup, bread and coal. In addition, casual giving to beggars was common throughout the land.

In the nineteenth and early twentieth centuries the role of the government was very limited by today's standards. Thus local tragedies or catastrophies were dealt with by private, unofficial

too much is done for those who make no effort to help themselves

charitable action. A hard winter, an epidemic, a colliery disaster, depression in local industry, all of these sparked off local collections of money, gifts of food, fuel and clothing. When, for instance, 168 miners were killed in a disaster at West Stanley, County Durham, in 1909 a vigorous local-relief campaign to help the wives and children of the men lost underground was started. Charity at all points over-lapped with the Poor Law. It provided hospitals, orphanages, almshouses for the elderly, homes for the handicapped, refuges for prostitutes, aid for widows, for the unemployed and so on. National charities which still exist today and do valuable work like the National Society for the Prevention of Cruelty to Children, and Barnardos were founded in the Victorian period. But it was local charities that were most vigorous. A survey carried out in 1862 showed that in London there were 640 charitable institutions (423 of them set up since 1800), and by 1885 there were approximately a thousand. The same picture can be seen in every city and town in Britain. For instance in Leominster in the early 1870s, a wealthy philanthropist set up an Orphans' Press to provide local orphans with training and experience in printing. In Newcastle in 1897, thanks to two local industrialists who each gave £100,000, the Royal Victoria Infirmary moved to new buildings. But surely the greatest philanthropist of the nineteenth century was the Scots-American steel millionaire Andrew Carnegie, who gave away $350 million to help the needy in Britain and the USA by building libraries, colleges, parks and swimming baths.

It has been estimated that total charitable giving in Britain in the nineteenth century was probably double that of France, a country which had no public service on the scale of the English Poor Law. One historian has calculated that in 1874–5 nearly £4 million was raised by organized charities in London alone. In the same year Poor Law expenditure for the whole of England and Wales was about £7½ million. However, some people did begin to feel that this huge amount of charitable giving was not being used in a completely beneficial way. In order to prevent overlapping and competition between different charities, and to ensure that help went only to those who deserved it, a body called the Charity Organization Society (COS) was set up in 1869. According to a magazine of the time, the COS felt that 'One chief cause of poverty is that too much is done for those who make no effort to help themselves.' The Society was firmly attached to the idea of people standing on their own feet, and carefully vetted each application for help to find out not just how much assistance was needed but also the worthiness of the applicants. Perhaps unsurprisingly, the COS was unpopular with many of those it sought to help.

However, by the late nineteenth century, a large number of working-class people were 'saving for a rainy day'; eight million were investing in Friendly Societies, which provided them with an income if they were ill, and many were subscribing to voluntary hospitals so as to ensure treatment when required. However, a large proportion did not earn enough to save, even when they had jobs. At best they lived literally on the breadline. For them there was little choice but the Poor Law system, especially in hard times. By the 1880s and 1890s more and more educated people were coming to see that private charity and the Poor Law had not solved the problem of poverty: much more state action was needed.

Two girls begging. What circumstances do you think would have driven the girls onto the street? What 'occupation' might they have turned to when they were older?

Religion and Charity

To the unsophisticated Christian, even of the nineteenth century, almsgiving was essentially a religious exercise, a manifestation of his love of God, of his obedience to the commands of his Lord and Saviour. 'Give unto every one that asketh thee', 'Sell all that thou hast and give unto the poor', were perhaps counsels of perfection impracticable for the householder with family responsibilities, and fit only for the saint whose entire life was dedicated to the service of God. Yet this universal and unquestioning yielding up of personal possessions for common consumption was thought to be the ideal conduct; the precious fruit of divine compassion. The spirit of unquestioning, of unrestricted – in short of infinite – charity was, to the orthodox Christian, not a process by which a given end could be attained, but an end in itself – a state of mind – one of the main channels through which the individual entered into communion with the supreme spirit of love at work in the universe.

Can you detect any signs in this extract that Webb is being sarcastic? What arguments against private charity might a socialist put forward?

From My Apprenticeship *(1926) by Beatrice Webb (1858–1943). The author came from a well-to-do family. She involved herself in charitable work as a young woman and helped Charles Booth in his famous survey of London poverty. By the time she came to write her autobiography she was a socialist.*

Can you see what charity these two boys are collecting for? The photograph dates from the end of the nineteenth century.

Self-Help

'Heaven helps those who help themselves' is a well-tried maxim, embodying in a small compass the results of vast human experience. The spirit of self-help is the root of all genuine growth in the individual; and, exhibited in the lives of many, it constitutes the true course of national vigour and strength. Help from without is often enfeebling in its effects, but help from within invariably invigorates. Whatever is done *for* men or classes, to a certain extent takes away the stimulus and necessity of doing for themselves; and where men are subjected to over-guidance and over-government, the inevitable tendency is to render them comparatively helpless.

Were there some people in the nineteenth century who were not able to help themselves? Is this also true today?

From Self-Help *(1859) by Samuel Smiles (1812–1904). The author produced several best-selling books in which he argued that those who worked hard and saved could make something of themselves.*

Charitable Institutions

Wigton Convent of Mercy, Carlisle; St Joseph's Home, Darlington; Lancaster Asylum; Border Counties Home, Carlisle; St Peter's Home, Gainford; St Mary's Home, Tudhoe; Hospital of St John, Scarton; Storthes Hall Asylum, Huddersfield; Edgeworth Children's Home, Bolton; Sunderland Boys Industrial School; *Wellesley* Training Ship; Green's Home for Boys; Shotley Bridge Training Home for Girls; Deaf and Dumb Institution, Newcastle; Blind Institution, Newcastle; York City Asylum; Beverley Asylum, Doncaster; Balby House, Doncaster; Dr Barnardo's Home, Ilford; Field Heath House, Middlesex; Leatherhead School for the Blind; Stoke Park Colony, Bristol; Midland Counties Institution, Chesterfield; Middlesbrough Asylum; Sedgefield Asylum.

Try to work out which groups of paupers might have been sent to these charitable institutions (for example, girls, boys, women, men, the elderly, the sick). What does this source tell us about the way the Poor Law had developed by 1914?

In one year before 1914 the South Shields Poor Law union sent deputations of workhouse guardians to check that its dependants were being well treated in the above institutions.

1 **Write for information to some charities working to relieve suffering and poverty in Britain today. You might be able to help these organizations through fund-raising events in your school. The address of Barnardos is:**

**Tanner's Lane
Barkingside
Ilford
Essex IG6 1QG**

The address of the Child Poverty Action Group is:

**1–5 Bath Street
London EC1V 9PY**

2 **Are there any charitable institutions such as almshouses in your area? Ask at the local-history section of your nearest big library whether any of the local hospitals began as charitably financed institutions.**

3 **Can you explain why a historian who believes in private property and private enterprise and a historian who is a socialist and believes in equality and in the public ownership of industry would probably disagree about the motives of men who gave large sums to charity in the Victorian period?**

4 **Imagine you are a wealthy Victorian. Explain why you propose giving a large sum of money to a charity.**

▲

A Salvation Army women's shelter in Whitechapel, East London, as shown in the Illustrated London News. *The Salvation Army was founded in 1878 by William Booth (1829–1912). It offered the poor a mixture of religion, cheerful services led by brass bands, and social welfare. Why do you think destitute women would prefer this grim-looking hostel to the workhouse?*

To throw some light on how the 1834 Poor Law system worked, let's look at its operation in two very different parts of England – Cornwall and the East End of London.

In the late nineteenth century Cornwall had a population of just over 320,000. It was still a poor, remote part of England, only gradually opening up to tourists. Its main industries were farming, fishing and the mining of tin and copper. However, both agriculture and mining were going through a difficult period and there was much poverty for the Poor Law authorities to deal with.

By this time the poor-relief system was supervised by a government ministry called the Local Government Board (the

Poor Law Commission had been abolished in 1847 and replaced by the Poor Law Board until 1871), but the country was still divided into about 700 Poor Law unions. Each union consisted of between ten and fifteen parishes, and the workhouse was usually built in the largest town in the union. Cornwall was divided into thirteen Poor Law unions.

A very useful source of information about life in Cornwall in the nineteenth century is *The West Briton*, the county's leading newspaper of the time. It reported on the scandals of paupers' funerals and on such casual brutality as (in October 1898) the unauthorized use in the Bodmin workhouse of a 'black hole' in which inmates were imprisoned

A Salvation Army band. Why do you think the Salvation Army has military-style uniforms and ranks? Why are brass bands a feature of the organization?

for misbehaviour. The great majority of articles in, and letters to, the newspaper make it very clear that the Poor Law was deeply unpopular with ordinary folk. However, a less gloomy story was reported in February 1885. A successful Cornish emigrant to New Zealand sent five frozen sheep carcasses as a present to the poor in one of the county's workhouses!

The only thing the East End of London had in common with Cornwall was widespread poverty. With its population of 450,000 the East End was a crowded, urban and industrial area. Cornwall certainly had its slums, both in the countryside and in the towns, but they could not compare in extent with what a historian describes as the East End's 'network of narrow streets, courts and alleyways, with off-shoots often ending in rook-eries: a maze of rabbit warrens, mainly topsy-turvey, one storied, leprous, grey-bricked hovels'. Charles Booth discovered that 35% of the people in this area were living con-stantly on or below the mar-gin of subsistence. Many men worked in the docks, a precarious livelihood as too many chased too few jobs, and work was on a casual basis and badly paid when available. Women and children worked in the sweated tailoring trade, labouring for long hours for very low pay.

In 1878 William Booth founded the Salvation Army to relieve distress and promote evangelical Christianity amongst the poor. Booth's famous book *In Darkest England and the Way Out*, published in 1890, vividly illustrates the poverty and suffering of the East End of London, in which he points out that there were 17,000 men, women and children in workhouses, asylums and hospitals. The Poor Law in the area was administered by six unions, who did their best to make sure that their workhouses were places of grim reputation.

In his novel *In Darkest London: Captain Lobo, Salvation Army*, published in 1889, John Law describes how even the Salvation Army was banned from holding meetings and singing hymns in London workhouses. In another of Law's novels, the central character, Jo, seeking shelter for the night, is put into the 'casual

ward', which consists of a series of grim, freezing-cold, cell-like rooms, 8 feet by 4 feet, each lit by a single jet of gas and containing no furniture except a thin mattress and a rug. In the casual ward, inmates are faced in their cells by large blocks of granite and a hammer. In exchange for

William Booth founded the Salvation Army to relieve distress amongst the poor

food and accommodation (supper consisted of a tin containing half a pound of gruel and 8 ounces of bread) they had in the morning, when they would have been better employed looking for work, to break half a ton of stone. No protective clothing such as eye-shields or strong gloves was supplied on the grounds that this was unnecessary and wasteful expenditure. If, like Jo, the inmate was unable to perform the work in full, he would be detained as a punishment for another day and a night, with an increase in the amount of stone-breaking expected of him. Jo was held for three days and two nights until a granite splinter flew into his eye. The workhouse master told Jo that if he returned within a month he would be kept for twice the time.

Workhouse records show that a sizeable proportion of long-term inmates in the East End workhouses were children. (Also maintained by the union were children living at home with their widowed mothers.) These workhouse children were mainly orphans or abandoned by their parents. One way of relieving the

rate-payers of the expense of supporting them was to encourage children to emigrate. In April 1888 the Whitechapel union sent orphans to Canada. The children, who were between the ages of nine and fourteen, were each given £11. Presumably in Canada they were to be fostered and set to work on farms. Another means of disposing of children was recruitment into the army or navy. In August 1888 the same East End union sent seven boys (four orphans, two sons of widows and one boy deserted by his father) to the naval training ship *Exmouth*. Another boy joined an army band. Children were 'boarded-out' to foster parents in country districts and this seems to have been popular with the 'pauper nippers' of Whitechapel. For girls, in particular, there was domestic service. London's north-west was then, and still is, an affluent area and there was a steady demand for servants. Boarded-out children of good character were often sent there after reaching the official school-leaving age. For instance on 18 September 1888 the union received a letter from the Rev. J. Bamber 'submitting proposals to place Caroline Carty, a poor child, boarded out under the care of that Committee chargeable to this Union, in the domestic service of Mr. Andre, 84 Mansfield Road, Haverstock Hill'. The Board of Guardians agreed and recommended that 'an outfit to the value of £3 be provided for Caroline'.

Despite some generous gestures by Boards of Guardians the operation of the Poor Law in England and Wales in the late nineteenth century was little more humane than it had been fifty years before. To enter the work-house was still the ultimate humiliation for the poor.

A Redruth Pauper

Some considerable amount of feeling has been shown by the poor people living at Plainangwarry, Redruth, on account of an old woman named Ann Bray, who died on the Saturday, and lay un-coffined until the following Thursday, when the parish coffin was brought in a donkey cart, and the old woman's body carried off therein to be buried at Treleigh. When the man with the corpse got there, there was no grave ready, and the old woman's corpse was left in the church porch for some hours alone, until the worthy vicar heard of the affair and ordered it to be interred, and it is hoped that an inquiry will be instituted into the conduct of those who are entrusted with the burial of paupers.

The West Briton, *27 December 1877*

What famous principles of the 1834 Act lay behind the old woman's treatment?

SUNDERLAND UNION.

REGULATIONS
RELATING TO THE
BATHING OF INMATES

1. All inmates are to be bathed at least once a fortnight (unless exempted by Medical Certificate), and oftener IF NECESSARY. Should there be any doubt as to the advisability of bathing any person owing to sickness, or other cause, immediate reference to be made to the Medical Officer.

2. The Bath Attendant ONLY is to prepare the bath, and during the bathing of inmates the bathroom must not be left without some paid Officer who is responsible for the conduct of the arrangements.

3. The COLD Water is to be turned on FIRST.

4. There must be 10 inches of Water in the Bath.

5. The temperature of the Water must be 98 degrees of heat. This is to be tested by the Thermometer (not by the HAND) before an inmate be allowed to enter the Bath.

6. Inmates are not to be kept in the Bath more than TEN minutes unless absolutely necessary, and on no pretence whatever are their heads to be put under Water.

7. NOT MORE than ONE Patient to be bathed in the SAME WATER.

8. After bathing, each inmate is to be dried and dressed as quickly as possible, and any bruises, wounds, or evidence of disease to be reported at once to the Medical Officer.

9. The KEYS are NEVER to remain on the BATH TAPS, nor are they to be used by patients. When not in use they are to be kept in the Attendant's Room.

10. The Baths, Floor, Brushes, Combs, &c., are always to be left in proper condition for next day's use.

11. Any deficiency in the supply of Warm Water, Soap, Towels, &c., to be reported.

12. All Wet Towels to be removed.

13. A printed copy of these Regulations shall be exhibited by the Master in the Bathrooms of the Institution.

By order of the Board of Guardians,

W. P. BRANTINGHAM,
Clerk to the Guardians.

APRIL, 1914.

Which of the rules show a wish not to spend too much money on the inmates? (NB Similar regulations governed London workhouses.)

Dining hall of the St Marylebone workhouse in London, 1900. The workhouse dining halls in the East End would have been very similar. Why are the men sitting in such a regimented fashion?

The Lambeth Workhouse

Although we were aware of the shame of going to the workhouse, when Mother told us about it both Sydney and I thought it adventurous and a change from living in one stuffy room. But on that doleful day I didn't realize what was happening until we actually entered the workhouse gate. Then the forlorn bewilderment of it struck me; for there we were made to separate, Mother going in one direction to the women's ward and we in another to the children's.

How well I remember the poignant sadness of that first visiting day: the shock of seeing Mother enter the visiting-room garbed in workhouse clothes. How forlorn and embarrassed she looked! In one week she had aged and grown thin, but her face lit up when she saw us. Sydney and I began to weep which made Mother weep, and large tears began to run down her cheeks. Eventually she regained her composure and we sat together on a rough bench, our hands in her lap while she gently patted them. She smiled at our cropped heads and stroked them consolingly, telling us that we would soon all be together again. From her apron she produced a bag of coconut candy which she had bought at the workhouse store with her earnings from crocheting lace cuffs for one of the nurses. After we parted, Sydney kept dolefully repeating how she had aged.

Why did Chaplin later become famous? Why were the two boys separated from their mother?

From My Autobiography *by Charles Chaplin (1964)*

1 Try to find out when your parish became part of a Poor Law union and where the union workhouse was. If it remains today you may find that it has been converted into a hospital. Your local main public library or museum may be able to help you.

2 If you live in East Anglia, see if you can visit the Norfolk Rural Life Museum, which is at Beech House, Gressenhall, Dereham NR20 4DR (telephone Dereham 860563). The museum is housed in the former workhouse of the Milford and Launditch union. Apart from the workhouse buildings (including a cell into which disobedient paupers were put) there is also the workhouse farm.

3 Read *A Child of the Jago* by Arthur Morrison (1896, republished 1982 by the Boydell Press). This is a novel about the East End of the 1890s, where crime and poverty are rife in an area with dreadful living and working conditions.

4 If you live in London you could perhaps visit the Ragged Schools Museum of East End Life, 46–50 Copperfield Road, Bow, London E3 4RR (tel. 081–980 6405).

The statistics gathered by the Poor Law authorities during the nineteenth century should have pleased rate-payers. The tougher post-1834 poor-relief system, together with a general rise in living standards from about 1850, seemed to have reduced poverty to a relatively minor problem, as the following figures suggest:

Year	No. of paupers on relief	% of population
1834	1.26 million	8.8
1850	1 million	5.7
1860	845,000	4.3
1870	1 million	4.6
1880	808,000	3.0
1900	792,000	2.5
1914	748,000	2.0

However, this picture of apparently declining levels of poverty was shattered by the work of social investigators like Charles Booth and Seebohm Rowntree from the late 1880s onwards. Their surveys, and others by Lady Bell, Mrs P. Reeves, William Booth, Jack London and Maude Davies, seemed to show that about 30% of Britain's population was living in poverty without help from the Poor Law authorities. The inadequate earnings of this large section of the population were supplemented by money, food and clothing from charities.

Although sensational and very influential in bringing about welfare reforms, the findings of Booth and Rowntree need to be used cautiously.

Charles Booth (1840–1916) was a wealthy Liverpool shipowner. He was provoked into starting his investigations into the extent of poverty by his annoyance at what he thought were exaggerated accounts of urban poverty, such as Andrew Mearns's *The Bitter Cry of Outcast London*, published in 1883, and the 1885 survey, published in the *Pall Mall Gazette*, carried out by a small, left-wing

Homeless and Hungry *by Luke Fildes (1874). A group of men, women and children queue for entry into the casual ward of a workhouse.*

political group, the Social Democratic Federation. These studies claimed that one-quarter of the East End of London's population was living in poverty. Booth (like the COS) believed that people should stand on their own feet; he also detested socialism. He decided to test his theory that there was less poverty than the SDF claimed by carrying out a survey of London with seven voluntary helpers. He also used information from the census reports and material provided by police records, education officials and Poor Law statistics. Booth's work took from 1889 to 1903 to carry out and his findings were published in seventeen volumes entitled *Life and Labour of the People in London*. Booth devised a minimum-income level, providing for the most basic needs of a family. This 'poverty line' enabled the extent of poverty to be measured fairly accurately. Booth also divided the population of London into eight categories, from A to H. The most famous figure thrown up by Booth's survey was that 30.7% of Londoners were living in poverty. However, the situation was not quite so alarming as it appeared and Booth himself was surprised at its impact. 'By the word "poor" I mean to describe those who have sufficiently regular though bare income, such as 18s. to 20s. per week, for a moderate family, and by the "very poor" those who from any cause fall much below that standard.' Categories C and D were the ordinary, unskilled working class, who did not starve but had to work for their daily bread. Only categories A and B were 'in want or distress' and unable to feed and clothe

themselves without outside help or the self-help of crime. They added up to not 'nearly a third' but one in twelve (8.4%) of London's population: the successors to the paupers of 1834.

Benjamin Seebohm Rowntree (1871–1954) was another businessman who also turned social investigator. Inspired by Booth's work, he carried out a very similar survey of his own

the Poor Law was largely ineffective in dealing with primary poverty

home town of York, which was published in 1901 and entitled *Poverty: A Study of Town Life*. Rowntree calculated exactly the weekly income needed for a family to maintain 'physical efficiency' (21s. 8d.) and concluded with what might seem absurd precision that 27.84% of York's population was living 'in poverty'. However, two-thirds of this figure were in 'secondary poverty', having just enough to live on if they did not squander it on drink, gambling or other non-necessities. Only one in ten (9.91%) in 'primary poverty' lacked sufficient income for bare physical efficiency and were truly below the poverty line, as Helen Bosanquet and Charles Loch of the COS pointed out. Perhaps Rowntree's most important contribution to the poverty debate was his idea of the 'poverty cycle', which showed that a person from the working class could move in and out of poverty during different stages of his life.

The most important feature of the work of Booth and Rowntree was not their claims for the extent of poverty so much as the light they shed on its causes. Rowntree showed that over half of the primary poverty in York was the result of low wages, with large families responsible for a further

20%. Another survey by A.L. Bowley in 1912, based on Reading, showed that almost half of children under fourteen were living below the poverty line. Sickness, particularly when it affected the husband, was estimated by Rowntree as the cause of over 20% of primary poverty. Booth's findings from the East End were as follows:

Old Age	32.8%
Sickness	26.7%
Drink	12.6%
Lack of work	4.4%
Other causes (especially low wages)	23.5%

By the start of the twentieth century it had become clear that people were poor not primarily because they were work-shy but because they were old, or ill, or unemployed, or members of a large family. If drunkenness was a factor in producing poverty it must be remembered that men and women drank alcohol to help them escape the awfulness of their daily lives. The surveys conducted at the turn of the century showed that the Poor Law was largely ineffective in dealing with primary poverty. The scene was set for the first steps towards what we call the 'Welfare State'.

Poverty in London

A (lowest)	37,610	or .9 per cent	In poverty, 30.7 per cent
B (very poor)	316,834	or 7.5 per cent	
C and D (poor)	938,293	or 22.3 per cent	
E and F (working class, comfortable)	2,166,503	or 51.5 per cent	In comfort, 69.3 per cent
G and H (middle class and above)	749,930	or 17.8 per cent	
	4,209,170	100 per cent	
Inmates of Institutions	99,830		
	4,309,000		

Graphically, the proportions may be shown thus:

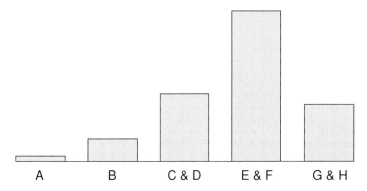

A   B   C & D   E & F   G & H

From Life and Labour of the People in London *(volume II)* by Charles Booth *(1892)*

How could you use these figures to back up the argument that poverty in London was a serious problem and how could you use the same figures to argue that poverty in London was a relatively minor problem?

"FREE TRADE"

An early twentieth-century postcard showing the alleged damaging effects of allowing foreign goods into Britain. Why do you think the family look so downcast?

Physical Efficiency

And let us clearly understand what 'merely physical efficiency' means. A family living upon the scale allowed for in this estimate must never spend a penny on railway fare or omnibus. They must never go into the country unless they walk. They must never purchase a halfpenny newspaper or spend a penny to buy a ticket for a popular concert. They must write no letters to absent children, for they cannot afford to pay the postage. They must never contribute anything to their church or chapel, or give any help to a neighbour which costs them money. They cannot save, nor can they join sick club or Trade Union, because they cannot pay the necessary subscriptions. The children must have no pocket money for dolls, marbles, or sweets. The father must smoke no tobacco, and must drink no beer. The mother must never buy any pretty clothes for herself or for her children, the character of the family wardrobe as for the family diet being governed by the regulation, 'Nothing must be bought but that which is absolutely necessary for the maintenance of physical health, and what is bought must be of the plainest and most economical description.' Should a child fall ill, it must be attended by the parish doctor; should it die, it must be buried by the parish. Finally, the wage-earner must never be absent from his work for a single day.

If any of these conditions are broken, the extra expenditure involved is met, *and can only be met*, by limiting the diet; or, in other words, by sacrificing physical efficiency.

Do you think that the COS would have been prepared to help the sort of family Rowntree is describing in this source?

From Poverty: A Study of Town Life *by B.S. Rowntree (1901)*

1 Draw bar charts for the statistics on the number of paupers getting Poor Law relief between 1834 and 1914 *and* for Booth's findings on the causes of poverty in London. Which way of presenting the information do you find most useful?

2 At what level would you set a poverty line today? Would you want to provide just for physical efficiency or would you be more generous?

3 The lives of ordinary people before the First World War are recalled in three splendid autobiographies: *The Classic Slum* by Robert Roberts (1971), about the author's childhood in Salford, near Manchester; *My Part of the River* by Grace Foakes (1976), set in the East End of London; and *My Autobiography* by Charlie Chaplin.

4 If you were a journalist today, what deprived groups of people might you investigate?

The Poverty Cycle

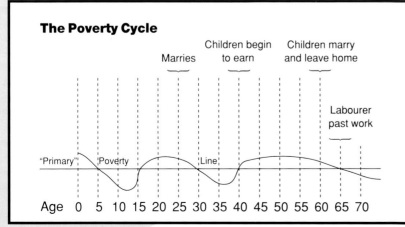

From Poverty: A Study of Town Life *by B.S. Rowntree (1901)*

This graph shows the periods of poverty and comparative affluence in the life of a working-class man. Can you explain why he is better or worse off at each different stage?

For most of the nineteenth century most educated people in Britain believed that governments should play only a very small role in running the economy and in providing social services. Politicians like William Gladstone and Lord Salisbury believed that poverty should be tackled through private charity, with the workhouse for the utterly destitute. Yet despite a widely held belief in 'individualism' and 'voluntaryism', Victorian governments by the end of the century had assumed powers to control pollution, to prevent food being tampered with, to provide elementary schools, to limit the hours worked by women and children in factories and to improve public health. Gradually,

and sometimes reluctantly, prominent men began to realize the scale of the country's problems and to appreciate that voluntary efforts were not enough to overcome them.

There were a number of reasons for this change of direction. One was the growth by the early twentieth century of working-class political organizations like the new Labour party and the Trades Union Congress, both of which had extensive social-reform programmes. By 1906, when the Labour party won twenty-nine seats in Parliament, about 60% of adult men had the vote. Another factor was the riot by unemployed men in London in 1886, which created widespread alarm among

Women making shells in a munitions factory during the First World War. Munitions work was one of the many new job opportunities for women at this time. Although it was dirty and dangerous, the pay was good.

the wealthy. Perhaps more important was the fear of many influential people that Britain was declining economically relative to the USA and Germany. To maintain the country's economic and political position 'national efficiency' was needed. The revelations about the poor health of many army volunteers for the South African War of 1899–1902 (in Manchester, for example, 12,000 men volunteered but only 10% were judged medically fit to serve) caused people like Sydney Webb and the leading Liberal H.H. Asquith to argue that national strength depended upon a healthy nation. 'What is the use of talking about Empire if here, at its very centre, there is always to be found a mass of people, stunted in education . . . huddled and congested beyond the possibility of realizing . . . either social or domestic life?' asked Asquith. The work of Booth and Rowntree was taken a step further by the University Settlement movement, which brought undergraduates from the middle and upper classes, like William Beveridge and Clement Attlee, to live and work among the poor of the inner cities and to experience conditions about which they would have otherwise remained completely ignorant. The 'New Liberals', radical young men like David Lloyd George and Winston Churchill, were affected by these factors and were keen to involve the Liberal party in social reform. As Lloyd George said, 'In so far as poverty is due to circumstances over which man has no control, then the state should step in to the very limit of its resources.'

In the thirty years before 1914 both the Conservatives and Liberals extended the role of government in dealing with poverty. Thus in 1886 the President of the Local Government Board, Joseph Chamberlain, instructed Poor Law unions to find useful work for the unemployed that would not label them as paupers. In 1905 the Unemployed Workman's Act gave local authorities the right to create work at the rate-payers' expense, thus removing the threat of the workhouse from many people. But it was the years 1906–14, when the Liberal governments led by Sir Henry Campbell-Bannerman and H.H. Asquith passed a mass of social

legislation designed to tackle the problem of poverty, that many historians think marked the birth of the Welfare State. The first steps taken by the Liberals, the provision of school meals in 1906, school medical inspections in 1907, and the Old Age Pensions Act of 1908, were all reforms that had been widely discussed for a number of years. By contrast, those after 1908, spearheaded by Lloyd George and Winston Churchill, pushed into new territory. The scandal of sweated labour was tackled through the Trade Boards Act of 1909, which tried to regulate wages in low-pay industries like tailoring. The Labour Exchanges Act of the same year created a national network of offices through which the unemployed could seek work. The most important piece of legislation was the National Insurance Act of 1911, part one of which covered most employed people against the financial consequences of sickness, disablement and maternity. The second part of the Act dealt with un-employment. Benefits were to be paid for fifteen weeks to over 2 million workers in jobs liable to short periods of unemployment, such as ship-building, engineering and building. Both parts of the Act were financed through weekly contributions paid by employees, employers and the state.

Although the Liberal social reforms before 1914 are often described as laying the foundations of the Welfare State they did not represent a clean break from the past. The structure of the Poor Law was still left to act as a safety net for those whom the Liberal reforms did not cover. Yet the 1834 Poor Law system

was itself clearly in need of reform by the start of the twentieth century.

Attempts at such a reform by a Royal Commission, which reported in 1909, had got nowhere when the First World War broke out. Far from the war increasing poverty by interrupting trade, as some people had feared, the massive demand for labour to create and equip huge armies drove up wages. One million women entered the workforce and some young women who before the war would have got 5 or 6 shillings a week in domestic service were earning 20 to 30 in munitions factories. Life expectancy for civilians increased during the war as people were able to afford more food, and the gradual introduction of rationing from 1917 ensured a fairer distribution of this food. In order to increase production of war materials, conditions in factories were improved and limit-ed opening hours intro-duced for all public houses. The government paid separation allowances to wives whose husbands were in the army or navy, and pensions to war widows and disabled ex-servicemen. By 1920 these payments were costing the government twice as much as old-age pensions and unemployment benefit paid under the 1911 National Insurance Act. The numbers on poor relief fell dramatically and it seemed that the Poor Law would not survive the war. In the general election held in late 1918 the Prime Minister, Lloyd George, promised 'To make Britain a fit country for heroes to live in.' But the Poor Law system was to last another thirty years.

'To make Britain a fit country for heroes to live in'

Lloyd George on Poverty

I do not think the better-off classes, whose comfort is assured, realize the sufferings of the unemployed workmen. What is poverty? Have you felt it yourselves? If not, you ought to thank God for having been spared its sufferings and its temptations. Have you ever seen others enduring it? Then pray God to forgive you, if you have not done your best to alleviate it.

By poverty, I mean *real* poverty – not the cutting down of your establishment, not the limitation of your luxuries. I mean the poverty of the man who does not know how long he can keep a roof over his head, and where he will turn to find a meal for the pinched and hungry little children who look to him for sustenance and protection. *That* is what unemployment means . . .

From a speech made at Swansea on 1 October 1908 by the Liberal Chancellor of the Exchequer, David Lloyd George

Would you accept Lloyd George's definition of poverty today or would you want to increase the range of this definition?

'Address to Lloyd George, M.P.'

Lloyd George o' aul age pension fame,
Guids blessin's on yer honoured name;
There's nae anither ane we'd hail,
Apairt frae Royal George himsel',
Wi' prooder, heartier, kindlier cheer,
Or Heilan' welcome mair sincere.

Nae matter though ye played a pliskie
And raised the price o' Heilan' whisky,
We'll tak a dram o' sma' dimensions
And think upon oor auld age pensions;
Ye ken we like them baith guid measure,
But frien', the pension is the treasure.

Two verses from a poem written by a well-known local poet, Alexander Birnie, to mark Lloyd George's visit to King George V at Balmoral in 1910

This poem is written in the local dialect of north-east Scotland. Can you put it into your own words? Note Lloyd George had increased the taxation on whisky!

BRINGING DOWN THE HOUSE.

Mr. Lloyd George (responding to calls of "Author!" after the first performance of his great Insurance Drama). "Never knew the haloes come so thick before. Pit and gallery I'm used to, but now the stalls and dress-circle have broken out!" [May 17, 1911.]

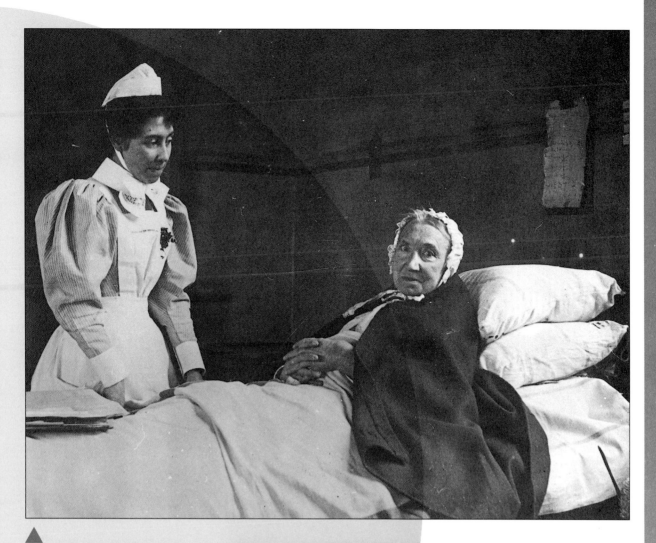

An old lady in a Manchester workhouse at the start of the twentieth century. What evidence does this photograph contain of a more humane attitude towards the elderly poor?

A cartoon from Punch, 17 May 1911. Try to explain the caption. Do you understand the references to 'Pit and gallery' and 'stalls and dress-circle'?

1 Using the sources in this and previous chapters write a letter to a newspaper from an old-age pensioner in January 1910.

2 Make a list of the causes of the welfare reforms carried out by 1918. Try to put these causes into the following categories: political or social or economic; long-term or short-term.

3 The sources used in this chapter are favourable to the Liberal welfare reforms of 1906–14. But not everyone welcomed them. What sort of people were likely to oppose these social reforms, and what primary sources could you look at that might give a different picture of them?

4 Try to borrow from your school or public library Flora Thompson's well-known book *Lark Rise to Candleford* (1945). Find the section that describes how elderly villagers reacted to getting their first pension payment.

TO-MORROW – WHEN LABOUR RULES

The picture many people still have of the 1920s and 1930s is one of depression, deprivation and decay, of dole queues, hunger marches, slum houses, malnutrition and bitter class and industrial relations. However, the inter-war period was not marked entirely by dismal failure and widespread unrelieved poverty. To quote just one example: turnover in Marks and Spencer's shops, despite the economic depression of the time, multiplied nearly ten-fold between 1929 and 1939. This suggests that prosperity and the possession of increasing amounts of consumer goods were also a feature of this period.

The novelist J.B. Priestley in his classic travel book of 1934, *English Journey*, pointed out that there were three Englands. First was the 'Old England' of ancient cities like York, Norwich, Durham and Warwick, which had a faded prosperity. Then there was 'nineteenth-century England', made up of declining industrial areas such as South Wales, North-West and North-East England, Northern Ireland and Central Scotland, based on industries like cotton, iron and steel, ship-building and coal-mining. Finally there was the 'new post-war England' of London, the Midlands and the South-East, which was expanding and prosperous. It was in 'nineteenth-century England' that inter-war poverty was concentrated, for it was here that unemployment had risen rapidly after 1918, due to increasing competition from abroad. A Labour government elected in 1929 pledged to conquer unemployment, but almost immediately the world

Labour election poster, probably from 1918. The first Labour government was elected on a programme of social reform in 1924.

sank into the 'Great Depression', sparked off by the Wall Street crash of October 1929. As the USA went into deep economic depression, Europe followed suit.

Unemployment in Britain was higher between the wars than before 1914, never dropping below a million; it should also be remembered that the workforce was much smaller then than now, partly because the total population was smaller and partly because fewer women went to work. As a result of the Wall Street crash there were 2 million out of work by July 1930 and nearly 3 million by late 1932. However, for many workers between the wars unemployment was a temporary set-back, and most were out of work for less than six months. The real problem lay with the large number of long-term unemployed, mostly middle-aged men in the old industrial parts of Britain. Thus, even in a boom year like 1937, the rate of unemployment in a depressed area like South Wales was over 22% compared with 6 or 7% in London, the South East and the Midlands.

Poverty between the wars was at the same time much reduced compared with that of the late nineteenth century, yet it still existed on a scale and to a degree that shocked middle-class Britain when it was forcibly brought to its attention by the evacuation of verminous working-class children during the Second World War. In a second survey of York in 1935–6, Rowntree, using a higher minimum standard than the one he had used in 1899, found only 6.8% of the total population living in primary poverty (compared with 15.8% in 1899), but as he pointed out there was little room for complacency. If 43% of the working class in York lived in poverty (primary or secondary) in 1899, 31% were still in this state by 1935–6.

Rowntree found that the causes of poverty remained much the same as before 1914. Although the number of workers covered by National Insurance against unemployment had been extended in 1920 to 11 million, by 1938 (when it stood at 15.4 million) it provided a weekly sum of money equivalent to only 45–66% of average former wages, varying according to age. This figure meant that most

Poverty still existed on a scale and to a degree that shocked middle-class Britain

recipients could live only in poverty. In addition, large families had difficulty staying above the poverty line. There was no child benefit and Rowntree consequently found that over half the working-class children in York were born into poverty. What made inter-war poverty so obvious was its concentration in certain parts of the country, in the areas of declining industries already listed. One 1934 estimate suggested that nearly 80% of breadwinners in South Wales earned less than £4 a week, compared with 68% in London and the South East. To look at this another way: in 1936 Brighton had only 3,000 unemployed compared with Oldham's 15,000, yet the two towns had roughly the same size of population.

The poor naturally lived in the worst housing, and large numbers of slums still existed. A survey of 1933 revealed that in London alone half a million people were living in overcrowded conditions. Outside London every large town and city had its slum areas. In central Liverpool 42% of families lived more than four families to a house, and in 1932 there were still one hundred families living in cellars. In 1943 nearly 40% of the houses in Hull and 90% in Stepney in East London were without baths and 12% of Birmingham's houses in 1946 had no separate lavatories.

The poor, of course, suffered the worst health. Although the health of the nation improved considerably between the wars, with the expansion of medical services and better diets (e.g. the infant-mortality rate for England and Wales was 105 per 1,000 in

1910 and 46 per 1,000 in 1940), there were significant differences in health levels according to people's social class. Thus the death rate in England and Wales for men aged between twenty and sixty-four in professional jobs in 1930–2 was 10% below the average, while for unskilled labourers it was 11% above. The infant-mortality rate for middle-class children was 33 per 1,000 live births, compared with 77 per 1,000 for the children of unskilled workers. The reasons for the poor health of the working classes were unsurprising: they could not afford medical care; bad housing conditions endangered their health; low incomes meant poor diets; and unemployment itself reduced a family's life expectancy. Remember also that until the National Health Service was set up after the Second World War, all persons not covered by National Insurance (as wives and children were not) or by private insurance had to pay cash for medical treatment.

For those in employment, the 1920s and 1930s were a period of increasing prosperity. Wage earners were earning as much as 30% more in 1938 than in 1913, and food prices had fallen. It became rare to see bare-footed, ragged children. Cigarette smoking greatly increased and consumer goods like radios and vacuum cleaners became common. Millions of people each week went to the cinema, filled in football coupons and went dancing. Twenty million people a year were enjoying a holiday by the sea in the late 1930s.

By 1939 the majority of Britons were wealthier than ever before but a sizeable minority still lived in poverty, a poverty made all the more noticeable because of most people's affluence.

Men Without Work

How many per 1,000 workers were unemployed for a year or more in the summer of 1936?

Men Only

1	Coal-miners	123
2	Ship-builders and repairers	95
3	Cotton workers	67
4	Seamen	59
5	Pig-iron and Iron and Steel workers	57
6	Pottery and Earthenware workers	54
7	Workers in Textile Bleaching, Dyeing, etc.	37
8	Waiters and other workers in Hotels, Public houses and Restaurants	33
9	Gas, Water and Electricity workers	33
10	Boot and Shoe workers	31
11	General Engineering	31
12	Dock and Harbour workers	27
13	Workers in Distributive Trades	27
14	Workers in Bread, Biscuits, Cakes, etc.	26
15	Workers in Tailoring firms	25
16	Builders and Building Labourers	24
17	Furniture workers	21
18	Printers, Bookbinders	14
19	Workers in Motor Vehicles, Cycles, etc.	10
	All Workers	41

From Men Without Work, *a report by the Pilgrim Trust (1938)*

The Pilgrim Trust was founded by public-spirited men in Great Britain and the USA in 1931 and gave grants of money to voluntary groups trying to help the unemployed. Can you place any of these various types of occupations in the geographical areas shown in 'Unemployment'? Which of the above industries do you think were in decline in the 1930s?

Unemployment

Percentage of Insured Workers Unemployed in Distressed and Prosperous Towns, 1934

Jarrow	67.8	Greater London	8.6
Gateshead	44.2	Birmingham	6.4
Workington	36.3	Coventry	5.1
Maryport	57.0	Oxford	5.1
Abertillery	49.6	Luton	7.7
Merthyr	61.9	High Wycombe	3.3
Greenock	36.6	St Albans	3.9
Motherwell	37.4	Watford	7.0

Can you find these towns on a map of Britain? Which regions of Britain were most affected by unemployment?

From Britain between the Wars 1918–1940 *by C.L. Mowat (1968)*

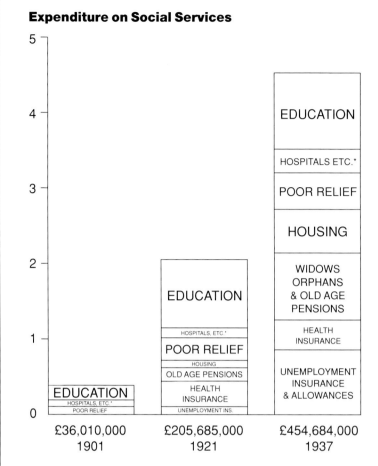

Expenditure on Social Services

EDUCATION

HOSPITALS ETC.*

POOR RELIEF

HOUSING

WIDOWS ORPHANS & OLD AGE PENSIONS

HEALTH INSURANCE

UNEMPLOYMENT INSURANCE & ALLOWANCES

EDUCATION

HOSPITALS, ETC.*

POOR RELIEF

HOUSING

OLD AGE PENSIONS

HEALTH INSURANCE

UNEMPLOYMENT INS.

EDUCATION

HOSPITALS, ETC.*

POOR RELIEF

£36,010,000
1901

£205,685,000
1921

£454,684,000
1937

*Hospitals and treatment of disease; mental welfare and, from 1921, maternity and child welfare

Which categories of spending in 1921 and 1937 helped the fight against poverty?

From The British Social Services *by A.D.K. Owen, first published 1940*

1 Draw a map of Britain. Put on it the towns listed in 'Unemployment' and write in beside them the percentage of unemployed in 1934.

2 Which of the jobs in 'Men Without Work' would you expect to find in 'Old England', 'nineteenth-century England' and 'new, post-war England'?

3 Imagine you are a schoolteacher. Make up a list of questions that will show whether your pupils understand the source material in this chapter.

4 A famous book which is well worth dipping into is George Orwell's *The Road to Wigan Pier* (1937), which describes the mines, unemployment, slums and malnutrition of the coal-producing areas of Lancashire and Yorkshire. *Growing Up in the Gorbals* by Ralph Glasser (1986) tells of the author's life in the Glasgow slums before the Second World War.

Moving through the silent crowd
Who stand behind dull cigarettes,
These men who idle in the road,
I have the sense of falling light.

They lounge at corners of the street
And greet friends with a shrug of shoulder
And turn their empty pockets out,
The cynical gestures of the poor.

From a poem written in the 1930s by Stephen Spender

Can you devise a caption for this photograph and a title for the poem above?

An ex-serviceman busking in a London street, c. 1927. What do you think this man would have felt at being reduced to a street performer?

The Arrival of the Jarrow Marchers in London *by Thomas Dugdale (1936). What attitude is shown by the man and woman in this painting?*

Governments in the 1980s and early 1990s have not found it easy to tackle the problems of high levels of unemployment nor to deal with continued poverty. This should perhaps stop us condemning too quickly the governments of the inter-war years for their failures in these areas.

After the end of the First World War many people thought that problems at home should be tackled with the same vigour with which the war had been fought. For a short while after 1918 the economy boomed and much was done to improve housing and pensions and help the unemployed. But then from 1920 through to 1939 Britain was plunged into economic difficulties. In 1921 and again in 1931 governments felt they had to cut their spending and not spend more than they received in taxes. Higher taxes were thought to be bad for business, which in turn meant higher unemployment. More radical ideas for ending the depression were being developed during the 1920s by the economist John Maynard Keynes, who was beginning to argue that governments should increase their spending, but most ministers and civil servants thought this would make matters worse. Their general view can best be summed up by the Conservative election slogan of 1929: 'Safety First'.

Yet steps were still being taken to tackle poverty, and in 1929 the Local Government Act, piloted through Parliament by the Conservative Minister of Health Neville Chamberlain, struck a great blow against the Poor Law. The 635 unions designed to serve the needs of a largely uneducated and voteless population had lingered on into an age of mass education and universal suffrage. By now, thanks to the pre-1914 welfare reforms, the role of the workhouse was declining, and inmates were mostly elderly or physically and mentally ill. But unions faced an increasing burden in dealing with the growing numbers of unemployed. In March 1921 there were 224,000 on outdoor poor relief, and by June 1922 over one million. Moreover, this burden fell unevenly on the system, with about two hundred unions in the poorest parts of the country coping with the majority of unemployed people. This meant that in these areas the poor rates were very heavy: twenty-five times higher in depressed Gateshead than in prosperous

Blackpool. To try to solve this problem the government decided to abolish the unions and hand over their powers to the town and county councils. Each local-authority area would have a Public Assistance Committee responsible for the poor.

In effect the Poor Law had collapsed under the pressure of mass unemployment, as it was politically impossible to impose on the unemployed the humiliation of poor relief through the workhouse. But the 1834 system had also been undermined by the growth of National Insurance. Although the 1911 National Insurance Act had covered workers in just three trades, between 1920 and 1934 another twenty Acts of Parliament extended this scheme to nearly all workers. By 1931 unemployment benefit (set at about one-third of the average wage) was costing so much money that the government, faced with an economic crisis, cut it and introduced the hated 'means test'. By 1934, as the economic crisis eased, the government was able to restore the cuts. The unemployment insurance scheme now covered 15 million workers. Employers, workers and the state contributed equal amounts to a central fund, out of which benefits were paid – normally for a maximum of twenty-six weeks – during unemployment. A married man also received benefit for his wife and children.

However, there was a second line of defence for the unemployed man. Workers who exhausted their right to insurance benefit could apply for unemployment assistance. This had been introduced in 1921 to provide help for the poor without the shame of applying to the Poor Law system. These 'transitional payments', as they were known, were from 1931 subject to a means test. Before they could get

financial help, claimants had to declare all forms of income, including pensions, savings and contributions from sons, daughters or relatives living with the family. If a man's son had a newspaper round or his wife a few pounds in the Post Office Savings Bank, he had to declare these details and his 'dole' would be reduced. By early 1932 almost a million unemployed were registering for the dole but large numbers of claims were disallowed. For instance, in Lancashire only about 16% were awarded the full dole, while a third of claims were completely refused. In the first year of operation £24 million was saved, but at a high cost in suffering and ill-feeling. As the writer George Orwell put it, the means test was 'an encouragement to the tattle-tale and the informer'. If a child whose father was on the dole was seen with a bicycle or a new coat, the 'means-test man' would soon get to hear about it and call to inquire where it came from.

In 1934 the Unemployment Act replaced the PACs with a central body, the Unemployment Assistance Board, which finally, after hundreds of years, removed from local control responsibility for the able-bodied poor. But the amount of dole (after National Insurance assistance had run out) continued to depend on a means test, which although a little less severe than before was still regarded by the poor with disgust.

Most long-term unemployed men lapsed into inactivity and depression. Some, however, took part in 'hunger marches' between 1922 and 1936, one of which has extended into the popular historical memory. This was the

the marchers even had their unemployment benefit stopped

march of 200 unemployed men from Jarrow, a ship-building town in North-East England, in 1936. The Jarrow 'crusade', as it was known, was organized by the local Labour MP, Ellen Wilkinson, and the town council, in order to draw attention to Jarrow's 80% unemployment. The good spirits and dignity of the marchers attracted support from people along the route and from the newspapers. On reaching London in November they held a meeting in Hyde Park and presented a petition to Parliament. But the government refused to give aid to revive ship-building in Jarrow and the marchers even had their unemployment benefit stopped on the grounds that they were unavailable for work during the period of the march!

For many people in Britain the inter-war years were a period of misery and deprivation. Yet there was some progress in dealing with the problem of poverty. Even for people out of work, average unemployment benefit in the 1930s was higher than unskilled wages at the turn of the century. Old-age pensions had increased and pensions for widows and orphans were introduced; health insurance covered 19 million wage-earners by 1936; 2 million council houses were built in twenty years; the Poor Law had been transformed, and long-term unemployment relief introduced; there was also a growing public-hospital service. One might say that at the very least the framework of the Welfare State was in place. Moreover, the distress caused by mass unemployment had left a deep impression on middle-class people.

The Hidden Poor

When you see the unemployment figures quoted at two millions, it is fatally easy to take this as meaning that two million people are out of work and the rest of the population is comparatively comfortable.

This is an enormous under-estimate, because, in the first place, the only people shown on unemployment figures are those actually drawing the dole – that is, in general, heads of families. An unemployed man's dependants do not figure on the list unless they too are drawing a separate allowance. A Labour Exchange officer told me that to get at the real number of people *living on* (not drawing) the dole, you have got to multiply the official figures by something over three. This alone brings the number of unemployed to round about six millions . . .

From The Road to Wigan Pier *by George Orwell (1937)*

Do you know how many people are unemployed in Britain today?

A Tupp'ny Leanover

'Ain't y' heard? He's joined th' army cause he had to.'

'Had to?' repeated Harry.

'Aye, bloody well had to. His pa kicked him out o' th' 'ouse when he was knocked off dole. Told him t' clear out 'n join th' army cause he wasn't gonna keep him. He wus livin' i' one o' them doss houses i' Garden Place. Poor devil couldn't afford price of a bed. Tuk him all his time t' find for a tupp'ny leanover.'

Harry gazed at Jack, puzzled: 'Tupp'ny leanover. Wha' d'y' mean?'

Jack shrugged: 'Y' should go 'n have a luk at it. It's for t' real down and outs as can't afford price of a bed. They charge y' tuppence t' lean o'er a rope all night. Hell, y' should see 'em. About forty blokes sittin' on forms in a line an' leanin' o'er a rope . . . elbow t' elbow swayin' fast asleep, except the old bastards who're dyin' and can't sleep for spittin' an' coughin' their guts away . . .'

Can you explain what this extract from Greenwood's novel is about?

From Love on the Dole *by Walter Greenwood (1933)*

The Jarrow marchers pass through the village of Lavenden near Bedford on their way to London, 26 October 1936. Why did the marchers carry a banner describing their protest as a 'crusade'?

THE END OF THE TRAIL

From the Morning Post, *10 November 1936. Can you explain what point the cartoon is trying to make? What political party do you think this newspaper supported?*

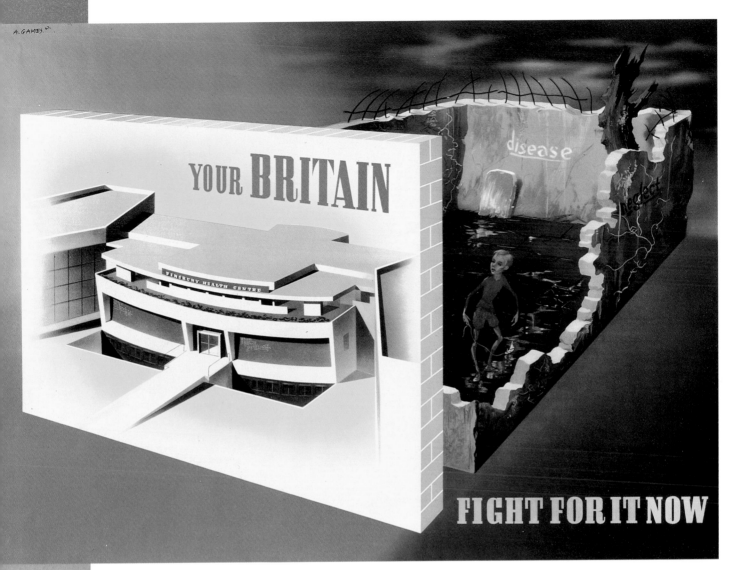

YOUR BRITAIN

disease

neglect

FIGHT FOR IT NOW

During the wartime years 1939 to 1945 the government controlled every part of life in Britain much more comprehensively than in 1914–18. By 1945 there were 8 million men and women in the armed forces and all civilians – except married women – between the ages of eighteen and sixty were directed into war industries. Government spending increased enormously, the civil service doubled in size and state supervision of everyday life extended even to the design and quality of clothing and furniture. The experience of total war sharpened the nation's awareness of social problems (for example, through the evacuation of children) and encouraged

discussion of them (for example, through adult education in the armed forces). Official reports were published on health, social security, education and many other matters, all of which drew a sharp contrast between the world before the war and the world as it might be. The very austerity of wartime, with rationing and shortages of all sorts of goods, meant an emphasis on 'fair shares for all'.

In 1937 experts calculated that in two months 600,000 people could be killed in air-raids. A massive evacuation programme was therefore put into effect in September 1939 when war did break out. Altogether about 3½ million children and mothers were

Your Britain: Fight for It Now (1944). What promises for the future are being made in this poster? Why do you think it was withdrawn by the government shortly after its release?

evacuated from large cities in 1939–41 and billeted on householders in the countryside. Many evacuees came from city slums and disliked the strange food and strict middle-class discipline of their hosts. Equally, many country people and well-to-do householders in small towns had no idea of how the poor lived in London, Birmingham, Liverpool and Glasgow. In many reception areas people reacted angrily to the influx of dirty children, but even before the end of 1939 some social workers were pointing out that the mixing of classes might provide a future basis for reform, since the extent of poverty in Britain could no longer be ignored.

Most foodstuffs (but not bread) were rationed from January 1940. Everyone had a ration book, and amounts varied according to the food-supply situation. By mid-1941 some weekly rations consisted of no more than what a respectable pre-war household would have thought sufficient for a single helping: 8 ounces of fats (including 2 ounces of butter), one egg, 2 ounces of jam and marmalade. Generally speaking, eating habits were standardized, with almost everyone now eating at the level of a prosperous working man of the inter-war years. This of course represented a great improvement for many and, although there was much queuing and much monotony in people's diets (most children never saw an orange or a banana), food subsidies and price controls meant that the cost of living was kept down. Thus rationing helped create a sense of equal sacrifice.

There was a dramatic decline in infant mortality during the war. In 1939 the rate of deaths of infants under twelve months per 1,000 live births had been 51 in England and 69 in Scotland. By 1945 the figures were 45 and 56 respectively. This improvement was due to the equalizing effect of rationing and to various government measures. In 1940 the Ministry of Health began a campaign to have children immunized against diphtheria, a fatal disease thought likely to spread among people crowded into air-raid shelters. A National Milk Scheme was also introduced in 1940, which provided free or cheap milk to all mothers and children. In 1941 cod-liver oil and orange juice were given free to children and expectant mothers. Many local authorities started providing subsidized school meals for all children. In 1940 the Assistance Board was set up, replacing the old Unemployment Assistance Board. It paid supplementary pensions to over one million old people and widows, aided bombed-out families, wives of dead service-men, elderly people who were separated from their families, and young children whose mothers were at work.

In June 1941 the government ordered a special Committee of Inquiry to undertake 'a survey of the existing national schemes of social insurance and to make recommendations'. Chairman of the committee was Sir William Beveridge, an experienced civil servant who turned this inquiry into an ambitious programme of social reform. He proposed a comprehensive system of compulsory social insurance to provide for all classes, and a minimum standard of living 'from the cradle to the grave'. In what was virtually a charter of human rights Beveridge argued that, if his scheme for a social-security system that was not means tested was to be workable, three related 'assumptions' must be brought into play: family allowances, a National Health Service and policies to prevent mass unemployment. The Beveridge Report came out in the autumn of 1942 in a blaze of publicity. It was the lead story in all the newspapers and the BBC broadcast news of it in twenty-two languages. Published shortly after the victory at El Alamein, the report came at just the right moment, when people's thoughts were beginning to turn to the post-war world. The report met with overwhelming popular

'fair shares for all'

support. One public-opinion survey showed that 86% favoured its adoption. Employers and the upper-middle classes were almost as strongly in favour as manual workers, and Beveridge became a national hero. However, some Conservative politicians were more guarded in their response to the report, as they were afraid of raising hopes that the country might not be able to afford to put into operation; Winston Churchill described Beveridge as 'an awful windbag and a dreamer'.

In July 1945, shortly after the end of the war, a general election was held. The Labour party fought a powerful campaign based on the creation of a Welfare State and on the nationalization of key industries like the railways and coal, and on economic planning. Churchill tried to frighten the electorate with talk about the dangers of socialism, warning that its introduction into Britain would require 'some form of Gestapo'. When the results came through it was clear that Churchill's tactics had misfired. Labour won a landslide victory with 397 seats to the Conservatives' 197.

Historians argue about the extent to which the war changed Britain. However, there can be little doubt that the 'People's War' on the home front, with the 'Blitz' in 1940–1, evacuation, rationing and the total mobilization of the population and the nation's economic resources to fight Germany and Japan, helped prepare the way for a post-war period of increased state intervention in social affairs and the creation of what many people saw as a more equal society. Yet poverty was to be harder to eradicate than people had hoped in 1945.

Evacuees

Apart from this major accusation of uncleanliness, there are other facts disclosed in this book which indicate that parents in the poorer classes are ignorant of the simplest principles of child welfare. It was found, for instance, that many people were totally indifferent to the importance of sleep. No habits of regular bed-time had been inculcated into the urban children, who were allowed to go to bed whenever they chose. Many parents appeared totally unaware of the basic principles of nutrition, and would spend money on sweets or comics which would have been far better devoted to the provision of food. It was found that many of the evacuated children had never sat down to a meal and did not know the use of forks or spoons. Their diet seems to have consisted almost exclusively of fish and chips, pickles, ice-cream and sweets; many of the children had never seen their mothers cook and had never had a hot meal at home. Vegetables to them were unknown and therefore distasteful. They regarded the country diet with suspicion and alarm. The remedies for these defects are obvious. They include housing, sanitation, water-supply, more day-nurseries . . . more hot meals in schools, better school premises in urban areas and, above all, education for parents in the elements of child welfare. The task is immense, but the disgrace is great. Bad conditions will not be remedied if we pretend that they are incidental, inevitable, or non-existent.

Harold Nicholson in The Spectator, *16 April 1943*

The Spectator *usually* **supports the Conservative party. Can you explain why it is significant that such a magazine should contain an article like this?**

After the War

There'll be work enough too, when this lot's over; building up something new and better than what's been destroyed. There mustn't be no more chaps hanging around for work that don't come. No more slums neither. No more dirty, filthy back streets and no more half-starved kids with no room to play in. We've got to pack all that up and get moving out into the brightness of the sun. We've got to all pull together.

An extract from a Ministry of Information film made in 1941

Why would the government make a film carrying a message like this during the Second World War?

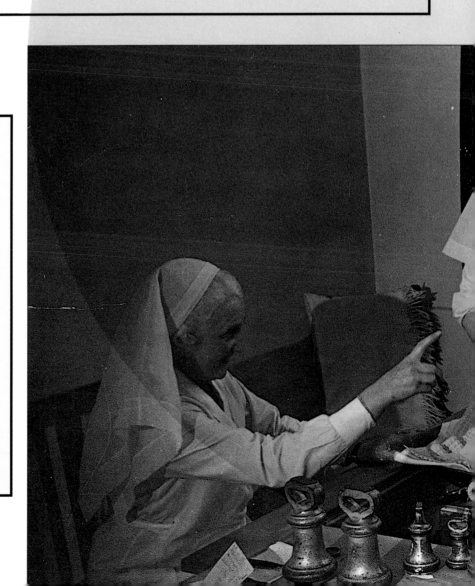

Critics of the Welfare State

I hope that Beveridge gets cut down. I am all for educating the people into being less awful, less limited, less silly, and for spending lots of money on extended education, but not for giving them everything for nothing, which they don't appreciate anyhow. Health, yes. Old age pensions yes, I suppose so . . . But not for this form of charity which will make people fold their arms and feel that they need have no enterprise since everything will be provided for them. It is a mistake.

Why does the writer think that very generous benefits are bad for people?

Extract from a letter written by Vita Sackville-West to her husband Harold Nicholson at the end of 1942

1 Write a short scene from a play in which Vita Sackville-West and her husband Harold Nicholson discuss the Beveridge Report.

2 Do some research on the evacuation of children and their mothers to country areas in the first months of the war. Two useful books you could consult are *How We Lived Then* by Norman Longmate (1971) and *The People's War* by Angus Calder (1969).

3 Write a brief biography of Beveridge. You will find information about him in most encyclopaedias.

4 Talk to older people about things like evacuation, rationing and the Beveridge Report. Record what they say and see whether it compares with what your school books say.

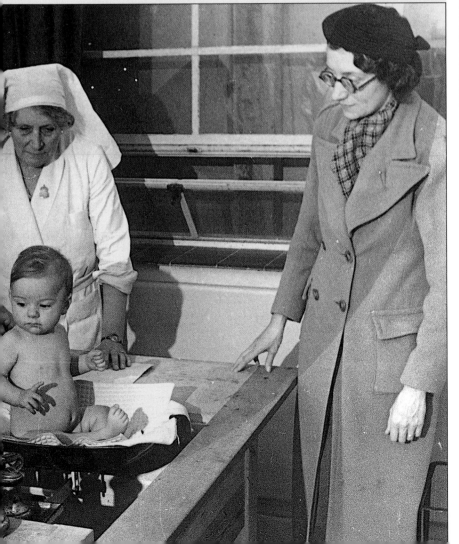

This photograph, originally published in Picture Post *on 29 July 1944, shows a scene at a health centre at East Finchley, north London. What does it suggest about the extent of health care before the setting-up of the National Health Service?*

Historians today agree that between 1945 and 1979 there was a high degree of consensus between the main political parties over a range of policies, including support for the Welfare State set up by Attlee's Labour government of 1945–51. 'Consensus' is Latin for 'agreement' and, although there were arguments between Labour and Conservatives, the policies pursued by the two parties when they were in office were quite similar. This consensus grew out of the

Harold Macmillan making an election speech at Greenford, Middlesex in 1959. Under 'Supermac' the Conservatives won the election with an increased majority.

experiences of politicians and ordinary people during the war, when there had been a sense of comradeship and a breaking down of barriers between the social classes. The political parties had shared power in a coalition between 1940 and 1945,

had agreed on the need for full employment after the war and had largely supported the Beveridge proposals.

The term 'Welfare State' had been widely used during the war to point a sharp contrast with Hitler's 'warfare state'. During and after the war it was increasingly believed that everyone in Britain had a right to the full range of social benefits (as opposed to the patchy pre-war system) as and when they needed them. This was the principle of 'universality' and three Acts of Parliament attempted to put it into practice. In 1946 the family allowance that your mothers draw each week from the local post office was introduced. This was a big step towards reducing child poverty. Even more important was the 1946 National Insurance Act, which set in place the main Beveridge proposals; all workers aged between fifteen and sixty-five (sixty for women) had to contribute what was then the sizeable amount of 25p per week in return for financial benefits paid to those suffering unemployment. Maternity and death grants were also paid, as well as pensions to all old people and to widows. The benefits were flat-rate (i.e. everyone got the same) and Beveridge had intended that they should be sufficient for the maintenance of a basic standard of living, but even in 1948 when the Act came into operation they had fallen below this level. Moreover, the individual contributions paid each week quickly proved to be insufficient to fund the system and the government was soon having to give millions of pounds from taxes to balance the books. In 1948 the National Assistance Act finally abolished the remnants of the 1834 Poor Law and also set up the National Assistance Board, a continuation of the Unemployed Assistance Board of the 1930s.

This gave financial help to people like the self-employed and men on strike, who did not qualify for National Insurance payments, and to those for whom such payments were insufficient. National Assistance was usually only paid out after a needs test, which although it was not as harsh as the pre-war means test (e.g. it did not include a check on a claimant's family) still deterred many from applying for help.

The 1950s was a decade in which the austerity and deprivation of the war and immediate post-war years were replaced by a growing prosperity in which more and more people were able to enjoy annual holidays, buy their own homes and fill them with televisions and washing machines. The Conservatives were in power from 1951 to 1964 and made little effort to alter the structure of the Welfare State they had inherited from Labour. In 1957 the Conservative Prime Minister Harold Macmillan made a speech in which he said that ' . . . most of our people have never had it so good. Go around the country . . . and you will see . . . prosperity such as we have never had in my lifetime – nor indeed in the history of this country.' In 1951 the elderly Seebohm Rowntree carried out a third survey of poverty in York. He found that the impact of the welfare reforms had been dramatic. Whereas before the war 31.1% of the population had been living in poverty, the figure now stood at only 2.77%. As the economy grew so did the amount of national wealth spent on social security. Between 1949 and 1964 this spending tripled while the cost of living 'only' doubled.

However, by the 1960s optimism that poverty could be eradicated was fading. It was clear that retirement still plunged many elderly people into poverty,

although they were now free of the threat of the workhouse and their diets were much improved. Even in the early 1950s, 25% of pensioners were claiming National Assistance because their state pensions were insufficient to maintain a basic level of existence. An added problem came with the slum-clearance programmes. As old, inner-city, working-class streets were demolished and people were rehoused in large council estates, the elderly were hit hard. As one old woman said in the mid-1950s: 'You notice the difference out here, when you fall on hard times. Up there where you were born, you could always get helped by your family . . . Down here you've had it.' Children were also still vulnerable to poverty. By the early 1960s the National Assistance Board was giving help to the families of 400,000 children.

Efforts to deal with such poverty in the 1960s and 1970s were hampered by the faltering economy. In both 1966 and 1976 Labour governments, led by Harold Wilson and James Callaghan respectively, faced severe financial crises. Despite these difficulties, governments, both Conservative and Labour, tried to improve social-welfare provision. In 1966 Labour passed a National Insurance Act which increased pensions and other benefits and introduced financial help for people made redundant. In the same year the Ministry of Pensions and National Insurance set up twenty years before was replaced by the Ministry of Social Security. National Assistance was renamed Supplementary Benefit in an effort to remove the shame some people felt at claiming help from the government. Edward

Heath's Conservative government in 1971 passed a Social Security Act introducing Family Income Supplement, which was targeted at low-income families. Then in 1975 a Labour government led by Harold Wilson passed two Acts, one of which improved old-age pensions, while the other replaced family allowance with Child Benefit and also provided help for unmarried mothers and separated parents with children.

Critics of the attempts by governments to tackle poverty in the 1960s and 1970s were particularly angered by the 'Wage Stop' regulation, under which benefits were paid at a lower rate than the wage earned by a person when last in work. This was designed to stop people 'scrounging' off the Welfare State, but it often led to a 'poverty trap', under which a family already on a low income was even worse off when existing on Supplementary Benefit.

The years 1945–79 saw great strides taken in the battle against poverty, with the Conservatives and the Labour party in broad agreement on the methods that should be used to tackle it. But as the cost of the Welfare State grew and as poverty obstinately remained, so the consensus came under strain. Increasingly, some Conservatives argued that welfare benefits should be targeted at those most in need rather than, for instance, giving all mothers, rich and poor, family allowances for their children.

'. . . most of our people have never had it so good'

THE WELFARE STATE

From Punch, *1949*

Can you explain the point the cartoonist is trying to make? Who is the 'John Bull' figure in the pram meant to represent?

Family Allowance

My son, aged nine, was rather peeved that his younger brother, aged nine months, should qualify for the new 5s. family allowance, so we agreed that each should get half. There being some delay before we were able to collect our first payments I was able to place two certificates each to my two sons' credit in their War Savings accounts, and we shall continue to do this, so that they will have the benefit of the money when they are older.

What might a critic of family allowances have said on reading this magazine article? (No benefit was paid for the family's first child.)

Picture Post, *16 November 1946*

▶ **A welfare worker helps an elderly man. What sort of form might they be filling in?**

Slum Housing

It's damp, and the roof's falling in. The back bedroom's no good to sleep in, you can't sleep in that. The four of us have to sleep in one bedroom. A little girl, a little boy, me husband and meself. We've got a lavatory outside, no bathroom, cold water, got no hot water at all. I wouldn't know what a bathroom looked like. Nine people share the toilet with us. It's disgraceful. The wall's knocked down between the two toilets and you still can't go in if there's somebody in the next one. You've to wait until they're both empty, because you can see one another, you know. You sit side by side . . . like that. Nobody wants that, do they? And the rats there – you have to dodge them. They get a bit rifely.

Extract from 'Northern Slums,' a BBC Archive disc dating from the late 1950s. (Quoted in The Long March of Everyman, *ed. T. Barker, 1975)*

Do people live in conditions like this in Britain in the 1990s?

Making Ends Meet

I come away with about £15 at the moment – four days – sometimes I'm on three. I was on three last week, which is only about £14. And I've got to give my wife £10 for grub and rent, £1 a week for electricity, £1 a week for gas, is £12. Thirty bob for the travelling, and of course I've got to pay the Union, and all the other different things – that takes a shilling here and a bob there. I'm left with about £1 a week to entertain me and the wife, and it costs me – if I go down to the Club on a Sunday night, it costs me about £2. 10. So I'm in debt, really. Don't smoke, have a drink, have a wee bid on the horses and that. No bank book, nothing in the bank. I have no car – I haven't enough money to buy a car. I've been married five years and we've never been on holiday yet.

From 'More Equal than Others', a BBC Archive disc dating from the early 1960s. (Quoted in The Long March of Everyman)

Was this man 'poor'?

Two Nations

Despite the growth in national wealth the age-old inequalities remain. The position of the poor has improved. But, so, too, has that of the rich.

From Unequal Britain *by Frank Field (1973)*

Do you think that if some people are 'rich' then other people must, by definition, be poor?

Mrs Blackwell, a worker in the Lilac Cotton Spinning Mill at Shaw, near Oldham, Lancashire, receives treatment from a chiropodist (1947). The chiropodist visited once a week at the mill, which also had a nursery for the workers' children. Do you think the National Health Service should provide free treatment of this kind?

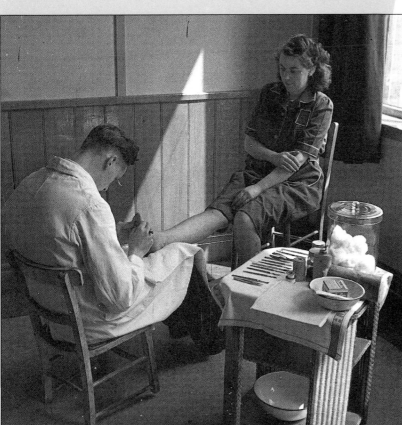

1 Ask older members of your family and their friends about life in Britain in the late 1940s, 1950s, 1960s and 1970s. Work out carefully the questions you want to ask them and tape-record what is said to you.

2 Find out from a teacher or an encyclopaedia how Parliament makes laws. Perhaps you might be able to visit Parliament yourself. Write to your MP and ask if (s)he can arrange this for you.

3 Pretend you are a cartoonist working for a newspaper which supports the setting-up of the Welfare State in the later 1940s. Draw a cartoon showing your pleasure at the actions of Attlee's Labour government.

It's Our Birthday

but
we're not
celebrating

CRISIS

25 YEARS

By the late 1970s social-security payments had narrowed the gap between those in and out of work to nothing at the bottom of the scale. Those caught in the poverty trap seemed to have little reason to try to get out. The Conservatives, under Prime Minister Margaret Thatcher, increasingly argued that the Welfare State was counter-productive, reducing those on benefits to a condition of dependence and calling new classes of idlers into being. Mrs Thatcher, who frequently stressed her background as a grocer's daughter from Grantham, called on Britain to 'Back the workers and not the shirkers', and talked of her belief in the 'Victorian values' of hard work, thrift and respect for authority.

In 1987 a television programme focussed public attention on what was called the 'underclass'. This, it was estimated, contained between 6% and 8% of the population and drew its numbers from the long-term unemployed, youngsters and adults, single-parent families and their children, and elderly people who relied on their state pensions. The lives of these people were characterized by poverty and criminal activity, by a breakdown of the family and a high rate of illegitimacy (10.6% of all live births in 1979, 25.6% in 1988). The members of the underclass were locked into a 'cycle of deprivation' – children born to poorly educated, single mothers will suffer in terms of health and education, will be involved in delinquency and then in crime and become feckless fathers or unmarried mothers;

Poster issued by the charity Crisis in 1992. Homelessness and poverty seemed to be increasing by the early 1990s.

thus the pattern repeats itself.

Until the 1970s the word 'Victorian' was rarely used in an approving sense. The Labour party echoed this attitude in its response to the increasing Conservative doubts about the Welfare State. Such doubts were 'un-caring' and showed 'callous indifference'. 'Victorian values', the Labour party said, meant the Poor Law, the workhouse, child labour and Dickensian slums. Throughout the 1980s the Labour opposition attacked Mrs Thatcher's governments for their abandonment of the post-war consensus on the need for full employment (the Conservatives argued that the battle against inflation had to take priority). Poverty was increasing, said Labour, and a DHSS report in 1990, which showed that average incomes for the poorest 10% of the population had fallen by 5.7% between 1979 and 1987 (while the level for the population as a whole rose by 23%) seemed to confirm that the poor were being excluded from a general rise in prosperity. Yet the paradox was that Mrs Thatcher made no effort to put these Victorian values into practice, certainly so far as the welfare system was concerned. No modern equivalent of the workhouse test was imposed on welfare claimants, and indeed the number of those depending on Supplementary Benefit rose from 3.4 million in 1979 to 5.6 million in 1988.

Busy with other problems and frightened of the electoral consequences of attacking the Welfare State head-on, Mrs Thatcher made only one attempt to reform the welfare system. The 1986 Social Security Act, which came into operation in 1988, was described by the government as

'Back the workers and not the shirkers'

the most radical reform of social security since 1942. The Act was designed to target resources on the most needy, to make the system simpler and easier to use, to encourage self-reliance on the part of those on low incomes and to try to reduce government spending. To achieve these aims, Supplementary Benefit was replaced with Income Support, and instead of special grants for a wide variety of needs, basic allowances were paid for families with children, single parents, pensioners, the long-term sick and the disabled. The system of Emergency Needs Payments which had grown up since the 1970s was turned into a single Social Fund, under which a smaller number of needs would be met by loans rather than grants. Family Income Supplement was renamed Family Credit and payments made through employers in order to try and increase the take-up rate, which was reaching only half of those who qualified. Finally, all claimants had to pay 20% of their community charge.

Even a radical reformer like Mrs Thatcher was able to make only a small impression on the vast social-security system. Conservative governments have not been able to roll back the Welfare State. With unemployment still high in the early 1990s the social-security budget has continued to increase. In 1989–90 it stood at £45 billion – 26% of total government expenditure. In May 1992 the government announced it was spending £70 billion a year on the needy. Yet still the problems seem to multiply, with one report published in 1990 claiming that 15 million people in Britain are living in poverty!

Margaret Thatcher's Childhood

I was brought up by a Victorian grandmother. We were taught to work jolly hard. We were taught to prove yourself; we were taught self-reliance; we were taught to live within our income. You were taught that cleanliness is next to godliness. You were taught self-respect. You were taught always to give a hand to your neighbour. You were taught tremendous pride in your country. All of these things are Victorian Values. They are also perennial values.

Margaret Thatcher in the Evening Standard, *15 April 1983*

Do you agree that these values are as relevant today as they were in Margaret Thatcher's childhood in the 1930s?

◀ *The People's March for Jobs on the road to Kilmarnock, 24 April 1983. What past event are these demonstrators consciously imitating?*

Life Expectancy at Birth

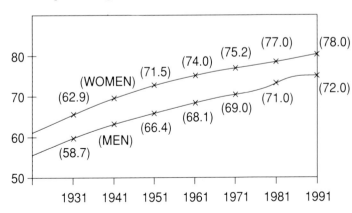

From Today in Darkest Britain *by C. Gaunklett (1990)*

These are average figures. What would a graph of life expectancy show for people living in poverty? Do you think this graph shows that poverty is diminishing in Britain?

The New Poor

'I juggle money about. If my daughter needs clothes I borrow from the gas money I've put aside and put it back later. I borrow off Peter to pay Paul.'

'Some days, especially on a Wednesday, I have to decide whether to go without sugar and get a loaf, or do without a loaf and get 2 lbs of sugar . . . I always get the bread, I think the neighbours will lend me a bit of sugar. You feel so small.'

'We've only got one electric fire in the lounge. The house is centrally heated but we got cut off two years ago due to arrears.'

'I'd like to give them more meat. The only proper dinner is Sunday, the rest of the time it's pizzas, burgers and things.'

'Often we have to go without meals at the weekend because there just isn't any money left. It's difficult when they're on holiday because I have to find an extra meal.'

'When he goes out for a drink he can't put his hand in his pocket and buy his mates a drink like they come and buy him one.'

From Missing the Target, *a report by Barnardos on the impact of the 1986 Social Security Act*

These are comments from families living in poverty. What evidence can you find of children living in poverty?

Measuring Poverty

An absolute standard of means is defined by reference to the actual needs of the poor and not by reference to the expenditure of those who are not poor. A family is poor if it cannot afford to eat . . . A person who enjoys a standard of living equal to that of a medieval baron cannot be described as poor for the sole reason that he has chanced to be born into a society where the great majority can live like medieval kings. By any absolute standards there is very little poverty in Britain today.

Keith Joseph (Conservative politician), 1976

Poor people in Britain are not, of course, as poor as those in the Third World. But their poverty is real enough nonetheless. For poverty is a relative, as well as an absolute concept. It exists, even in a relatively rich Western society, if people are denied access to what is generally regarded as a reasonable standard and quality of life in that society.

Can you explain what is meant by the phrase 'poverty is a relative, as well as an absolute concept'?

From Faith in the City *(a report by the Church of England on the inner cities), 1985*

1 Write to poverty pressure groups like Barnardos, Shelter, the Salvation Army and the Child Poverty Action Group and ask if they have any pamphlets or leaflets that would tell you about their work.

2 Have a look at the newspapers in your school library and collect articles on poverty in Britain today. Make a scrapbook of these.

3 Visit your local job centre and benefits office. Ask if they have any pamphlets on benefits that are available to people.

4 'Compared with Britain in the nineteenth century or Africa today there is no poverty in Britain.' Explain why you agree or disagree.

Milestones in the struggle against poverty:

1832 Royal Commission to investigate the Poor Law system set up.

1834 Poor Law Amendment Act – workhouses for paupers.

1908 Old Age Pensions Act – pensions as of right for those over seventy and earning less than the equivalent of £31.50 a week.

1909 'The People's Budget' increases taxes on the rich.

Poor Law Reports issued by a Royal Commission.

1911 National Insurance Act – insurance against sickness and unemployment for 2 million workers.

1914–18 First World War

1920 Unemployment Insurance Act widens Act of 1911 to include most workers and their families: 12 million people in all.

1925 Contributory Old Age, Widows' and Orphans' Pensions Act gives pensions to those over sixty-five.

1929 Local Government Act abolishes Poor Law unions and Guardians.

1931 Introduction of the means test – the 'dole' cut by 10%.

1934 Unemployment Assistance Board set up.

1939–45 Second World War

1940–5 Coalition government led by Winston Churchill.

1942 Beveridge Report

1945 Family Allowance Act

General election – Labour victory; Clement Attlee becomes Prime Minister.

1946 National Insurance Act – a new social-insurance scheme, covering the whole population 'from cradle to grave'.

1948 National Assistance Act sets up National Assistance Board to give extra money to those in need.

1966 Ministry of Social Security set up, replacing the National Assistance Board and the Ministry of Pensions and National Insurance.

1970 Equal Pay Act – designed to abolish the underpayment of women workers.

1971 Social Security Act introduces Family Income supplement to help the low paid.

1975 Social Security Pensions Act brings in a system of state pensions, consisting of a standard minimum and a supplement depending on wage when in work.

1979 Conservatives under Mrs Thatcher win the general election.

1986 Social Security Act replaces Supplementary Benefit with Income Support and brings in the Social Fund and Family Credit.

1987–8 Social-security spending costs £49.1 billion.

1992–3 Social-security spending costs £78.3 billion.

1993 The government announces that it is to carry out a thorough review of social-security spending (which amounts to 30% of all government expenditure), and plans to make drastic economies.

These photographs were taken in 1923 and 1987. What does it mean to be poor in Britain today? Do you agree with the Gospel of St John that 'The poor always ye have with you'?

45

able bodied   fit and strong; capable of working

absolute standard   an independent standard, one that does not depend on anything else

alleyway   narrow passage or street between houses or other buildings

almshouse   a house founded by charity for poor (usually elderly) people

asylum   institution for the shelter and support of the poor or ill (usually the mentally ill)

austerity   a comfortless and simple condition

Bastille   a prison in Paris destroyed in July 1789 during the French Revolution; workhouses were often called after it

billeting   the placing of evacuees or soldiers in a private house

Blitz   intensive attack from the air, especially as suffered by Britain in 1940–1

breadline   queue of poor people waiting for food. Those who live 'on the breadline' rely on charity to make ends meet.

Chartism   a mass working-class political movement which between 1838–48 campaigned for democracy. The name came from their 'People's Charter', listing the six main demands.

civil servants   the officials who work for government departments

community charge   a local tax introduced in 1990 to be paid by each adult; often called the 'poll tax'

comprehensive   including much or all

courts   spaces enclosed by walls or buildings, a number of houses enclosing a yard connected to the street by an alley

dependency   in a condition of being unable to manage without help from others

deprivation   not having a normal standard of living

destitution   being in extreme poverty

deterrence   a means to make people stop doing something

dole   a state payment to insured persons who cannot find work

El Alamein   a battle fought in Libya between British and German forces from 23 October to 4 November 1942, in which the Germans were defeated

elementary school   a school teaching reading, writing and arithmetic (usually to working-class children) before the Second World War

Friendly Society   a society for the mutual benefit of its members, who pay a weekly contribution, drawing an income from the society in times of illness or unemployment

flog   to beat severely with rod or whip as a punishment

Gestapo   the German secret police under the Nazi regime (1933–45)

gruel   a thick porridge made by boiling oatmeal in milk or water

individualism   the belief that people should prosper by their own efforts and stand on their own feet

infirmary   hospital

illegitimate child   one whose parents are not married

legislation   Acts of Parliament

leper   a person suffering from leprosy (an infectious disease affecting skin and nerves, resulting in deformities). The adjective is 'leprous'.

malnutrition   underfeeding

myth   an idea or a belief that is not based on fact

parish   the area served by a Church of England church. From the sixteenth to the nineteenth centuries parishes also played an important part in local government as the basic administrative unit of the Poor Laws

pauper   a very poor person who is receiving relief under the Poor Law

paymaster   an official who pays people, usually troops or workmen

philanthropist   someone who acts in a kindly and generous fashion because of a love of mankind

poor rate   a tax paid by householders to support the poor of the parish

radical   drastic, thorough, wide-ranging

rate-payer   someone who pays a local tax; the amount is based on the value of land and buildings

relative standards   those set in relation or proportion to something else

rookery   a crowded cluster of poor, broken-down houses

Royal Commission   a group of expert and important people asked by a government to investigate a current social or administrative problem

scrounger   someone wanting something for nothing, a beggar

shirker   someone who avoids work or carrying out his duty

slum   a dirty, overcrowded district inhabited by very poor people

socialist   someone who believes that land, transport, natural resources and the chief industries should be owned and managed by the state

Speenhamland system   the subsidizing of the wages of agricultural labourers from the poor rates, begun in the Berkshire village of Speenhamland in 1795. It soon spread throughout southern England.

squalor   dirt or unpleasantness, usually caused by neglect or poverty

sweated trades   industries such as tailoring and dressmaking, which were organized in the nineteenth and twentieth centuries in very small workshops and therefore escaped the controls on hours of work laid down by the Factory Acts

tuberculosis   often called TB. An infectious disease which particularly affects the lungs.

undergraduate   a university student

universal suffrage   all adults having the right to vote

voluntaryism   the belief that social services should be provided by volunteers and paid for by gifts to charities

Wall Street   site of the New York Stock Exchange

want   to be without the necessities of life

Further Reading

*T. Baker (ed.), *The Long March of Everyman*, BBC Books (1975)

R.C. Birch, *The Shaping of the Welfare State*, Longman (1974)

A. Calder, *The People's War: Britain 1939–1945*, Jonathan Cape (1969)

A. Digby, *The Poor Law in Nineteenth-Century England and Wales*, Macmillan (1982)

D. Fraser, *The Evolution of the British Welfare State*, Macmillan (1973)

*W.J. Fishman, *East End 1888*, Duckworth (1988)

*P. Henessy, *Never Again: Britain 1945–1951*, Jonathan Cape (1992)

*N. Longmate, *How We Lived Then: A History of Everyday Life During the Second World War*, Hutchinson (1988)

*N. Longmate, *The Workhouse*, Maurice Temple Smith (1972)

A. Marwick, *British Society since 1945*, Penguin (1990)

*C. Oppenheim, *Poverty: The Facts*, Child Poverty Action Group (1990)

*M. Rawcliffe, *The Welfare State*, Batsford (1990)

E. Royle, *Modern Britain: A Social History 1750–1985*, Edward Arnold (1986)

T.C. Smout, *A Century of the Scottish People 1830–1950*, Collins (1986)

T.C. Smout (ed.), *Victorian Values*, Oxford University Press (1992)

*T.C. Smout and S. Wood, *Scottish Voices 1745–1960*, Collins (1990)

J. Stevenson, *British Society 1914–1945*, Penguin (1984)

F.M.L. Thompson (ed.), *The Cambridge Social History of Britain 1750–1950*, vols 1–3, Cambridge University Press (1990)

D. Vincent, *Poor Citizens: The State and the Poor in Twentieth-Century Britain*, Longman (1991)

*J. Walvin, *Victorian Values*, André Deutsch (1990)

*R. Waters, *Edwin Chadwick, the Poor Law and Public Health*, Longman (1969)

P. Wood, *Poverty and the Workhouse in Victorian Britain*, Alan Sutton (1991)

*S. Wood, *The British Welfare State 1900–1950*, Cambridge University Press (1982)

*Books most suitable for schoolpupils

Acknowledgements

The Author and Publishers would like to thank the following for their kind permission to reproduce illustrations: e.t. archive, pp. 5, 24; Royal Commission of Historical Monuments, p. 7; Bridgeman Art Library, pp. 9, 16; Birmingham Reference Library, p. 10; Imperial War Museum, pp. 20, 32; Manchester Public Libraries, p. 23; Hulton Deutsch Collection Ltd, pp. 26, 27, 30, 34–5, 36, 39; the Geffrye Museum, p. 28; *Punch* Publications Ltd, p. 38; Central Office of Information, p. 38; Crisis (photo: Gideon Mendel/Network), p. 40; John Sturrock/Network, p. 42; Mark Power/Network, p. 43

The cover painting is *The Dole* by John Hodgson Lobley, reproduced by permission of the Bridgeman Art Library. The photograph shows a soup kitchen near Waterloo Station, London (© Neil Libbert/Network Photographers).

'Unemployed' by Stephen Spender is published in *Collected Poems 1928–1985*. The extract on p. 27 is reproduced by kind permission of Faber and Faber Ltd.

Thanks go to the *Changing Britain* series editors for advice and editorial input: Alan Evans and Michael Rawcliffe.